Build Your
Own Aviary

Build Your Own Aviary

A BIRDKEEPER'S GUIDE TO DESIGN AND CONSTRUCTION

D. W. Pearce

BLANDFORD

Blandford Press
An imprint of Cassell
Artillery House, Artillery Row, London SW1P 1RT

Copyright © Blandford Press 1983, 1989

First published 1983 by Blandford Press as
Aviary Design and Construction
This edition published 1989

Distributed in the United States by
Sterling Publishing Co. Inc.
387, Park Avenue South, New York, NY 10016-8810

Distributed in Australia by
Capricorn Link (Australia) Pty Ltd
PO Box 665, Lane Grove, NSW 2066

British Library Cataloguing in Publication Data

Pearce, D. W. (David William), *1941*–
Build your own aviary. — 2nd ed.
1. Aviaries. Design & construction
I. Title II. Pearce, D. W. (David William), *1941*–
Aviary design and construction
636.6'86

ISBN 0-7137-2150-2

Printed in Great Britain by Biddles Ltd,
Guildford and Kings Lynn

Contents

Acknowledgements

The author and publisher would like to thank Mr Sanderson of Southern Aviaries, Uckfield, Surrey, for permission to photograph examples of aviaries and also Miss Anita Lawrence for the line drawings.

1
The principles of aviary design

Bird-keeping is a hobby which has been enjoyed since the dawn of civilisation and it seems likely that the most important consideration — suitable accommodation for the birds — has been a problem since that time.

Birds are generally undemanding creatures and, given a proper diet, will thrive in the most unlikely aviaries, from the palatial and exotic to the ramshackle shed at the bottom of the garden. There is no doubt that, if the state of your finances allows it, one of the many proprietary aviaries on the market will provide excellent accommodation for your birds. These structures, however, may not meet your exact requirements. In addition, it is cheaper to build your own aviary and any money thus saved can always be spent on birds.

It is not a difficult undertaking and in this book I have attempted to set out the principles of aviary design and construction, not for the experienced carpenter, but for the average do-it-yourselfer. All the designs put forward require only basic tools, such as saw, hammer and drill. They are adaptable and will provide excellent accommodation for a wide range of species. The specialised accommodation required by some foreign birds, which range from the tiny humming bird to the biggest parrot is not considered as it is thought to be beyond the scope of the average bird-keeper.

First considerations

Having decided to build your own aviary, your first consideration must be its design. It seems almost inevitable that the newcomer to bird-keeping, fired with enthusiasm, builds a structure which is not

7

only unsuitable but also leaves little scope for future expansion. If you continue with the hobby, then expansion and alteration is certain. Careful planning and siting of your aviary, coupled with use of the most suitable materials, will save you frustration and expense in the years to come.

A trade-supplied modular-built aviary suitable for a small collection of seed-eaters or a single breeding pair

Materials

A brief discussion of the various types of building materials available should be helpful at this point. There is no doubt that a brick-built structure makes a very superior bird-room. This type of building is permanent, warm, dry and requires little maintenance. It is, however, its permanency that is the main disadvantage, apart from the very high cost of materials. Any modifications or additions to a brick-built structure are difficult and expensive. Also, there are few of us who do not move house at some time or another. You cannot remove a brick-built bird-room!

A practical solution is a clad timber-framed structure and a number of materials can be used for cladding.

Asbestos sheet has featured in a number of useful designs, but asbestos has several serious disadvantages. In the first place, the dust is dangerous, although the asbestos used in sheeting is not the very toxic blue variety. Secondly, asbestos sheet tends to be brittle and can crack quite easily given a sharp knock. Lastly, and by no means least, asbestos-clad structures tend to be hot in summer and cold in winter, although this effect can be minimised by effective insulation.

Exterior grade or marine plywood has much to recommend it. A bird-room clad in sheet material can be constructed with far less labour than one with the more usual timber planks. There is less chance of draughts with sheet material. In addition, exterior grade plywood is strong, durable and easy to maintain. There are, of course, drawbacks to the use of this material. It is more expensive than the equivalent area of tongue-and-groove board, extra members are needed in the framework to support the sheeting and, perhaps most important, its finished appearance is harsh and unattractive.

Oil-bound hardboard is another sheet material which must be given serious consideration. ¼ in (6 mm) exterior grade hardboard has a minimum life of ten years, which is quite adequate and compares favourably with most timber structures. Hardboard has all the advantages and disadvantages of plywood, but is cheaper. It is well worth considering if your budget is limited.

The traditional material for cladding timber buildings is either ship-lap or tongue-and-groove boards, most probably because these materials have proved to be the most satisfactory from every aspect. They are easy to use, durable and the finished structure is pleasing to the eye. It is for this reason, and as a result of my own experience, that I have specified tongue-and-groove boards (also known as 'matching') as the cladding material. There is, of course, no reason why any of the sheet materials specified should not be used, but this will entail strengthening the framework (see pp. 26 and 86).

Appropriate aviaries

Aviary requirements will vary according to the species of birds kept. For the sake of simplicity we can divide the categories into canaries, budgerigars, zebra finches, foreign and British birds.

The canary-fancier will usually only require a bird-room. Canaries, having been domesticated for several hundred years, live quite happily in cages and it is only rarely that an external flight is provided. The canary bird-room needs to be well lit and ventilated, allowance being made for tiers of cages on three walls.

Budgerigars ideally require a bird-room which contains two separate flights connecting with large external flights, plus a sufficient number of breeding cages.

Zebra finches require similar accommodation but on a smaller scale, i.e. the breeding cages and flights can be smaller. Two external flights connected to the internal flights are needed in order to separate the sexes.

When considering the type of housing to provide for foreign birds you must first decide on the scope of your bird-keeping activities. If it is your intention to keep a small, mixed collection of hardbills and softbills then you will need a well lit, heated bird-room with ample facilities in the form of cages and indoor flights. If you intend to breed from your birds then you will need a number of smaller flights, each with a suitable shelter. These remarks apply to the hardier varieties of seed-eaters and softbills. If you are considering aviaries for parrot-like birds, then you must take into account that parrots, both large and small, have extremely powerful bills. They are able to destroy woodwork and light gauge wire netting with surprising rapidity. In the majority of cases, parrot-like birds must be housed in individual flights, either singly or in pairs. If these flights are side by side, then the adjoining partitions must have wire netting on both sides of the framework to avoid the danger of injuries to feet, caused by parrots nipping their neighbour's toes as they cling to the wire netting.

To sum up, aviaries for most parrot-like birds should have individual flights, the size depending upon the size of the parrot, constructed from a substantial timber framework with heavy gauge wire netting. If possible, it is preferable to use steel angles for the framework, but this is probably beyond the capacity of the average handyman. It may be necessary also to protect the shelter woodwork with metal sheet in strategic places.

At the other end of the scale, we can consider housing for the more delicate softbills. These birds cannot endure much cold weather. The opportunity, due to a settled spell of fine weather, to allow them access to external flights does not occur often. The practical solution is to house them indoors. This is done very successfully by several zoos, bird gardens and private aviculturists, who provide accommodation in the form of large, planted conservatories but, again, this is considered to be beyond the scope of the average bird-keeper.

It is possible to maintain such birds in good condition in large flight cages and indoor flights but in these situations they are unlikely to breed and it is questionable, in today's climate of conservation, whether they should be kept in small private collections.

A trade-built ornamental aviary

Those who decide to concentrate on British birds will find that their choice of species is rather limited, those available usually being seed-eaters such as the greenfinch and linnet. These birds require an aviary with as large an external flight as possible, containing a small, dry, draught-proof shelter. During the breeding season, the rule is one pair of birds per flight and you must plan your range of aviaries accordingly.

Lastly, but by no means least, we come to those people who wish to have an aviary in their garden as a centre of interest, i.e. those who do not wish to become aviculturists in the true sense of the word, but want to keep a few birds as a relaxation for their family and themselves. An aviary for this situation must be practical, decorative and labour-saving. There is ample scope here for producing the unusual aviary which can fit in with a particular aspect of the garden and the octagonal aviary described in this book is a typical example of such a structure.

The question of aviary design can be complex, but, having discussed the general requirements for your chosen branch of the hobby, I hope to show you that the principles of design are common to each case and that any structure can be built up from similar basic modules.

2
Design consideration and layouts

There is no doubt that, from every point of view, aviaries constructed on a modular basis are the answer to most problems that arise in accommodating birds as this form of construction allows alterations and extensions to be made with ease.

In this context, a module refers to a standard-sized panel which can be clad in timber to form part of a bird-room or in netting to form part of a flight. There will, of course, be modules containing doors or windows and also roof and floor modules. These modules must be designed to make maximum economic use of the materials from which they are constructed.

Flight modules

In taking, as an example, a modular panel to form part of a flight, the first consideration is the overall dimensions of the panel. The height must be about 6 ft (1.8 m) to allow a person of average height to move around inside the flight without difficulty. This also allows full use to be made of the standard sizes of wire netting. The next problem is to decide the width of the panel. The purpose of the flight section of the aviary is not only to allow the birds ample flying space, but also to allow the birds to be seen. To allow maximum vision, the framework of the flight should be as unobtrusive as possible, while still providing a suitable structural strength. There are therefore two factors to consider, the width of the wire netting and the maximum distance possible between vertical members to give the necessary support to the netting. Wire netting comes in various widths. To make the best economic use of the netting we must avoid waste by using the full width. This will also minimise the amount of cutting required. I have found 3 ft (0.9 m) wide netting to be the size that best meets these requirements. The flight panel module will therefore measure 6 × 3 ft (1.8 × 0.9m).

Bird-room modules

Other factors must be considered for the bird-room or shelter section of the aviary. It is recommended that the framework of the module be clad in matching. This material places little restriction on the dimensions of the module, except that it is desirable to arrange the height of the module and the dimensions of any integral windows or doors to suit the width of the matching. For example, if the matching is 4 in (100 mm) wide then a module 6 ft 8 in (2 m) high will

A partially erected aviary showing the shelter section with pop-hole

need twenty lengths of matching. If the height were increased to, say, 6 ft 10 in (2.05 m) then one extra piece of matching would be required, 2 in (50 mm) wide. The amount of work involved in cutting a length of 4 in (100 mm) matching in half lengthways is not really worth the effort, apart from being a waste of timber.

The bird-room or shelter needs to be lined (see Chapter 3). One material commonly used for this is hardboard. The standard-sized sheet of hardboard, or similar material, measures 8 × 4 ft (2.4 × 1.2 m) This size is the factor in determining the width of the bird-room module in order to make the most economic use of materials. It is best to use the 8 ft (2.4 m) length vertically. This leaves the 4 ft (1.2 m) width as the controlling factor in deciding the width of the bird-room module. The answer is to provide vertical supports at 2 ft (0.6 m) intervals. The modules can then be constructed to any multiple of 2 ft (0.6 m) to suit requirements.

Doors and windows

Doors into bird-rooms and flights need to be given careful consideration as there is always the possibility of a bird escaping when you enter. This possibility is greater from the flight, but, even in the bird-room, a bird may have escaped from a cage. It has been suggested already that the distance between vertical supports should be 2 ft (0.6 m). This limits the width of the door to slightly less than 2 ft (0.6 m). While this may seem to be on the small side, I have found it to be adequate to allow removal of cages etc. Most importantly, it is narrow enough to allow the body to fill the gap when the door is opened. This is usually enough to discourage any loose birds from flying out. The entrance door of the flight is also small for the same reason, as will be seen by reference to the detailed designs (e.g. Fig. 15). The alternative is to build a safety porch, but this is an expensive project and tends to look unsightly.

The position and size of windows is always a difficult decision in aviary design. A bird-room or shelter must be well lit or the birds will either fail to prosper or, in the case of the shelter, will not enter. The position of the windows is important and is controlled by the use to which the bird-room is put. For instance, in the case of the canary bird-room, I stated that, preferably, cages should be placed against three of the four walls. This means that the fourth wall has to contain not only the windows, but also the door. Part of the same wall will be covered by the ends of the cages, which places further

restrictions on the space available for windows. There are a number
of solutions to this problem, some of which are shown in the detailed
bird-room designs. One which is not shown is the use of skylights or
windows in the roof of the bird-room as I consider these to be
difficult to construct and to keep watertight. They get dirty quickly
or, conversely, allow too much direct sunlight into the bird-room.
There is also the possibility that a fall of snow will cut off the natural
light altogether. Despite these disadvantages, many people have
used skylights successfully in their bird-rooms. If you have the skill
to construct them properly, and if your bird-room can be positioned
to avoid the full strength of the sun, then they are worth considering
in situations where maximum use of wall space must be made.

Economic layouts

Before considering the practical side of aviary construction it is as
well to give some thought to layout.

Let us take, as an example, the layout of an establishment for
budgerigars or zebra finches. In this case, two internal flights are
required, with access to external flights, plus a bank of breeding
cages. Provision should be made for storage of seed and equipment
if at all possible. There must be adequate room for the bird-keeper to
perform his usual bird-room activities, such as cage-cleaning, while
making maximum use of the space available to give the largest
possible flights and cages. I have assumed therefore that the
breeding cages will be 2 ft 6 in (0.75 m) or 3 ft (0.9 m) long by 1 ft (0.3
m) wide. The 2 ft 6 in (0.75 m) long cage may be considered a little on
the small side for budgerigars, but it is a size which is used
successfully and, as the emphasis of the designs in this book is on
economy it should be considered. I have taken as an example a 10 ×
6ft (3 × 1.8 m) bird-room, which is probably the minimum useful size
if you wish to breed exhibition birds. Figure 1 shows a very useful
layout. Two 6 × 2 ft (1.8 × 0.6 m) indoor flights are provided,
connected to two 9 × 6 ft (2.7 × 1.8 m) external flights. A block of
eight 3 ft (0.9 m) long breeding cages can be placed on the rear wall
between the flights. This allows for two windows (W) in the front
wall of the bird-room with the entrance door between them. Storage
space is available under the cages. If this area is insufficient for your
needs,then a raised floor can be fitted to the internal flights to give
extra storage area underneath. 30 ft^2 (2.7 m^2) of floor space is

available to the bird-keeper. This layout gives plenty of space, provides excellent accommodation for the birds and the arrangement of bird-room and flights gives a pleasing appearance to the aviary.

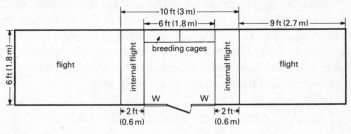

Figure 1 Aviary layout

Figure 2 shows the same bird-room and external flights with a different internal arrangement. The door and windows are in the same position, but the indoor flights are situated along the front wall of the bird-room. This layout allows for the provision of up to sixteen breeding cages, each 2 ft 6 in (0.75 m) long, in four tiers of four cages. Storage space is available under the cages and also under the flights, if required. This layout is quite useful if you require a large number of breeding cages. In order to gain the advantage of extra cages, you must accept the disadvantages of less inside flight area and less space in which to work. Although the available floor area for the bird-keeper is 34 ft^2 (3 m^2), a little more than in Figure 1, it is made up from a narrow corridor 3 ft (0.9 m) wide. While this is adequate, it does make cage-cleaning and access to the birds slightly uncomfortable. The lower breeding cages also tend to be rather dark, although extra windows in the end walls can overcome this problem. The external appearance of the aviary will be the same as in the previous example.

Figure 2 Aviary layout

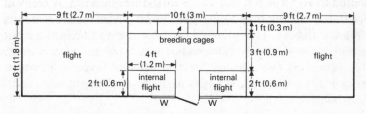

Figure 3 shows another possible layout. The sixteen breeding cages have been retained against the rear wall of the bird-room, but both inside flights have been moved to the front. This gives a larger area for the flights and also allows room for an extra window. The door has to be placed at the end of the bird-room, which means that one external flight has to be placed in front of the bird-room, as shown. Here again the working area in the bird-room is adequate, but rather cramped. The external appearance of the aviary is not as attractive as in the previous examples, but this layout may prove useful in some situations where space is limited.

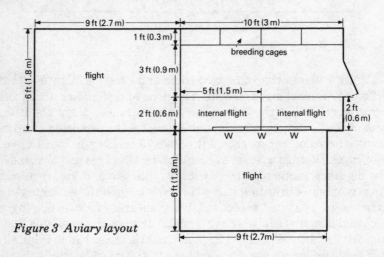

Figure 3 Aviary layout

A final permutation is shown in Figure 4. Two banks, each of eight 3 ft (0.9 m) long cages, face each other. Two small internal flights are placed side by side at the end of the bird-room. The external layout is the same as in Figure 3. This layout has several disadvantages and is only included to illustrate the many possibilities. The amount of window space is limited and two of the windows are partially covered by the breeding cages. It would be possible to provide windows at the end of each side of the bird-room, but this would mean that the walls of the inside flights would consist mostly of windows and it is not advisable to allow birds to roost against or near windows as these areas can be fatally cold during bad weather. This is one of the reasons for the window layouts on previous examples. In addition, the size and shape of the inside flights is unsatisfactory.

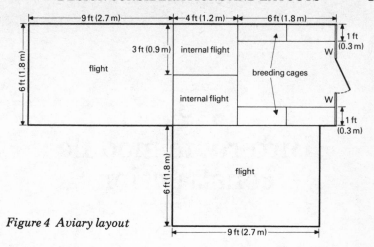

Figure 4 Aviary layout

Conclusions

The preceding remarks should give some idea of the considerations involved in designing an aviary. You will appreciate that the variations in design are almost without limit. It is the purpose of this book to set out the principles of design and to give some practical examples. The design of your aviary will probably be unique because no two sets of circumstances are the same. The detailed designs for aviaries and bird-rooms shown in the following chapters can all be adapted to suit your needs.

3

Bird-room module construction

Tools

There is no need for a vast range of tools when you come to construct your bird-room. The basic requirements are: a saw, drill, plane, tape measure, screwdriver, hammer, pliers, brad awl, paint brush, putty knife and, perhaps, a chisel and mallet. If you have a power saw and drill you can save yourself a fair amount of physical effort, but these tools are not essential.

Joints

To construct the modules, a timber framework must first be produced. This raises the question of how the members of this framework are to be joined together. I recommend 2 × 2 in (50 × 50 mm) timber for all the entire framework, both for bird-room and flight. This is quite strong enough for the purpose and, being square, simplifies the attachment of one module to another, particularly at the corners.

There are two methods of jointing the framework members. The first, and the most efficient, is by the use of half lap joints, as shown in Figures 5a and 5b. Figure 5a shows a corner joint. You will see that a piece is removed from the end of each member. In the case of 2 × 2 in (50 × 50 mm) timber this piece will measure about 1 in (25 mm) deep by 2 in (50 mm) long. An important point to remember is that the size stated is only nominal. Prepared or planed timber will measure about ⅛ in (3 mm) less than the stated size. Unfinished or sawn timber, which, incidentally, is cheaper to buy, should measure up to the stated size. No matter which timber you use, it is impera-tive that you measure it before cutting your joints. Measure twice before you cut is a good rule to adopt in woodwork. Once the ends of the timber have been shaped and tried for fit, the joint can be glued and screwed together. Use a waterproof adhesive, such as Casca-mite, with two wood screws per joint.

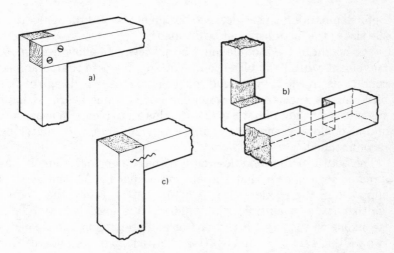

Figure 5 Methods of making joints: a) half lap corner joint b) half lap cross joint c) butt joint

Figure 5b shows a joint suitable for the situation where two members cross each other. Again, taking 2 × 2 in (50 × 50 mm) timber as the example, two saw cuts 1 in (25 mm) deep are made 2 in (50 mm) apart and a chisel is used to remove the required amount of timber. Both members are cut in the same way and checked for fit. The joint is then made as before.

The second method of making joints is shown in Figure 5c. This is known as a butt joint. The two sections to be joined are butted up against each other and the joint is secured, either with a corrugated fastener, as shown, or wood screws, plus adhesive. The corrugated fastener is quite an effective means of making a joint, although despised by the professional. The butt joint is not as strong as the lap joint, but once the cladding is in place on the framework, there is little to choose between them.

I would recommend the lap joint if you are prepared to make the effort. However, if your time is limited, or you are a little uncertain of your woodworking skills, then the butt joint is the answer. If you use corrugated fasteners, take care not to split the end of the timber.

Bird-room modules

Before embarking on the detailed design of the bird-room modules, the size of the modules must be decided.

The height of the module must be sufficient to allow freedom of movement within the bird-room. Nothing is worse than cramped conditions, in which your head touches the roof. The design of this bird-room is such that all walls can be the same height. I have suggested a height of 6 ft 8 in (2 m) as this gives plenty of headroom and also allows economic use of the 4 in (100 mm) wide matching recommended.

The width of the modules requires more consideration. It has already been shown that the optimum spacing for the vertical supports in the framework is 2 ft (0.6 m). Therefore the module width must be in multiples of 2 ft (0.6 m). It is possible to standardise on one width, say 4 ft (1.2 m) but more flexibility is obtained if two widths, 4 ft (1.2 m) and 6 ft (1.8 m) are adopted as standard. This course of action is recommended with the beginner in mind and also because the minimum practical width of bird-rooms is 6 ft (1.8 m).

Standard 6 ft (1.8 m) module

The 6 ft (1.8 m) module is shown in Figure 6. This illustration shows the principles which can be adopted for any size module. A door and window are included, but the module can be constructed with or without either.

The construction of the module is quite straightforward. The framework is assembled first from 2 × 2 in (50 × 50 mm) timber. The joints are made by one of the methods described.

Having made your framework, make sure that the corners are square and nail a piece of scrap timber diagonally across the corners to maintain this squareness while the matching is attached.

Next nail the matching in position, using two nails at each point where the sections of matching cross an upright. Do not forget the section above the window.

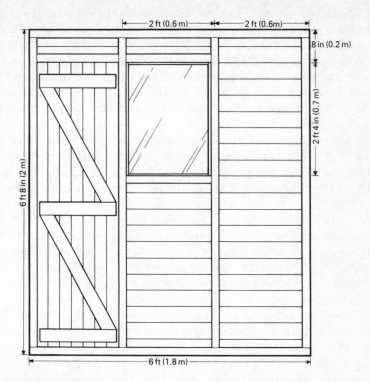

Figure 6 Standard 6 ft (1.8 m) wall module: view from inside

Door: The door can now be constructed. You will see by reference to Figures 6 and 7 that the matching for the door runs vertically and not horizontally as elsewhere on the module. The door is assembled around a 'double Z' framework constructed from 3 × 1 in (75 × 25 mm) timber.

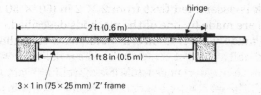

Figure 7 Section through door: view from above

The three horizontal sections of the framework are cut 1 ft 8 in (0.5 m) long. Place the three sections 2 ft 6 in (0.75 m) apart on a flat surface. Commencing from the left hand side, nail the first piece of matching into place. The top edge of the matching should be 6 in (150 mm) above the top edge of the upper horizontal section and the side should be 1½ in (38 mm) from the end of the section. This will allow the'Z' framework to clear the module framework when the door is closed.

Nail the rest of the matching in place, taking care to see that the top edge of the door remains straight, Check the squareness of the door and then measure off, cut and fit the two diagonal members. These act as braces to prevent the door from becoming distorted with use.

Figure 7 gives a plan view, i.e. a view from above, of the door. The dimensions given for the door should be checked against the dimensions of the module when it is constructed and allowance made for any inaccuracies in assembling the framework. Such inaccuracies can be enough to affect the fit of the door.

In the module shown, the door is designed to have the hinges on the left-hand side, when you face the door from the outside. This allows the surface of the door to be flush with the adjacent matching and gives the necessary overlap on to the framework at the opening side of the door. Two hinges will be quite adequate for a door of this size. They should be fitted so that the screws seat well into the door framework. If the hinges are positioned so that they screw into the matching, the screws will soon work loose.

Note that, in the module shown, a strip of matching 2 in (50 mm) wide must be fixed to one side of the window (see Figure 8) to bring the surface at this point up to the level of the door. The top hinge rests on this section and the screws must pass through it into the framework to provide a secure fixing.

Windows: The window can be either fixed or opening.

The fixed version is shown in Figure 8. The window frame is formed by the vertical and horizontal members of the framework. A window sill is provided by cutting a length of matching to fit in the position shown. This should have a groove on the underside to force rainwater to drip off. A suitable groove can be sawn or chiselled into the timber, but an efficient alternative is to fix a ½ in (12 mm) wide strip of hardboard to the front edge of the underside. This has almost the same effect as a groove.

Fitting the door hinge. Note the packing piece on the framework

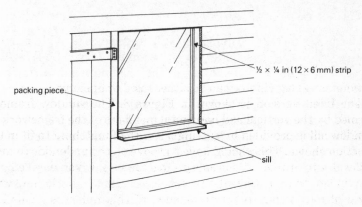

packing piece

½ × ¼ in (12 × 6 mm) strip

sill

Figure 8 Fixed window

A strip of ½ × ¼ in (12 × 6 mm) timber is then fixed to the inside of the frame, as shown in Figure 8 to provide a seating for the glass. If you wish to single-glaze the window, then fix the strip so that its rear edge is flush with the rear edge of the window frame. If it is your intention to double-glaze then the strip should be placed in the middle of the frame so that the glass may be fixed on either side.

Figure 9 shows the details of an opening window. The framework to carry the glass is made from 1½ × 1 in (38 × 25 mm) timber, positioned as shown. If you use lap joints at the corners, make them accurately and glue them properly, then the frame will give years of service. Should your joints leave something to be desired, then they can be strengthened by the use of steel corner plates, as illustrated. The dimensions of the window depend on the size of the opening in the framework when constructed. Measure the opening carefully and make the window frame ¼ in (6 mm) less overall than the size of the opening.

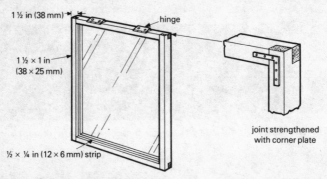

Figure 9 Opening window

The ½ × ¼ in (12 × 6 mm) strip still needs to be fitted to provide a stop and draught excluder for the window. The same size strip must also be fixed to the inside of the opening window frame to provide a seating for the glass. The remarks on glazing made for the fixed window also apply to the opening window, although, if you are considering double-glazing, you may need to substitute a ¼ × ¼ in (6 × 6 mm) strip for the ½ × ¼ in (12 x 6 mm) strip, in order to make room for the two sheets of glass.

The opening window is best hinged at the top, as shown in Figure 9. A window stay is required at the bottom to hold the window open. In all cases, do not glaze the windows until the aviary is erected or you may break the glass in the process of erection.

Pop-holes: One last factor, which must be mentioned when considering the construction of the wall modules, is the provision of an access-hole for the birds to fly from bird-room to flight. These are known by various names, such as bob-holes or pop-holes. Two arrangements for these access points are shown in Figure 10. Both arrangements are equally effective. In the first, a flap is constructed from the two pieces of matching removed when the hole was cut (Figure 10a). These are held together by two strips of timber, one at each edge. If the hinges are placed at the bottom, as shown, the flap will drop down to the horizontal position, where it will be supported by the ends of the strips, thus forming a landing platform. To close the opening, the flap is pushed up and held in place by a catch at the top of the hole.

The second method is to provide a sliding door (Figure 10b). This is a little more complicated to make, but does provide a more positive action. The door can be cut from hardboard, with pieces of scrap timber for a handle. A top and bottom track must be provided as shown in Figure 10b. This can be made from hardboard or any suitable pieces of timber. An end stop can be fitted, but this is not essential. Both methods require a framework of 2 × 2 in (50 × 50 mm) timber around the hole. This framework provides a fixing point for the matching and any lining fitted and also prevents the birds from gaining access to the gap between matching and lining.

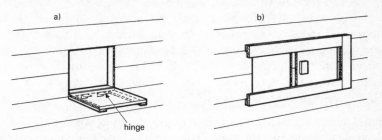

Figure 10 Pop-holes: a) with flap door b) with sliding door

Joining the wall modules: The best means of joining the wall modules together is to use ⅜ in (9 mm) diameter by 5 in (127 mm) long coach-bolts. Three of these should be used at each joint. At this stage of construction we must consider allowing access to these bolts when the lining is fitted to the module. To take the bolts, drill three holes in each end vertical member; these can be about 2 ft (0.6 mm) apart. Insert the bolts into the holes on one side of the module only and trap the heads by tightly screwing a piece of scrap timber over them. On the other side construct a box about 4 in (100 mm) square, made from 2 in × 2 in (50 × 50 mm) timber, around the hole. When the insulation material is put into the module, these boxes are left clear. Before the lining is fitted, squares are cut from the lining at these points to form lids for the boxes. These lids are screwed into position so that they may be removed to apply or remove the nut from the coach bolt, which will protrude through from the adjacent module.

Preserving the timber: Having assembled the module,the next step is to apply some form of wood preservative. However you decide to finish the exterior of your bird-room after assembly, it is important to ensure that all the timber is protected against rot and it is only at this stage that preservative can be effectively applied. Creosote or one of the proprietary brands of wood preservative may be used.The latter can be obtained in a number of different colours, so that you can give the woodwork an attractive finish and at the same time preserve it from rot. Apply the preservative to all surfaces, taking particular care with the lower part of the module, which is the most vulnerable area. Even if you wish to paint the exterior of the bird-room, it is still advisable to apply a coat of preservative, but in this case, the colourless variety should be used. Note that wood preservatives are toxic and the makers' instructions should be followed carefully. However, they have not been found to be dangerous to birds except before they have dried out. Creosote is the worst offender in this situation as it tends to burn if allowed to come into contact with the skin. Birds should not be allowed access to newly painted structures for at least three days, longer if weather conditions are not conducive to drying.

Lining and insulation: It is a great advantage to line the interior of your bird-room. The lining not only keeps out the draughts and provides an easy surface to paint, but also provides a surface with will act as the side or back of a breeding cage.

There are two materials suitable for lining bird-rooms. The more common and the cheaper is ⅛ in (3 mm) hardboard. The alternative is plastic-faced plywood wallboard, which is sold in a variety of wood effects. The latter may be a little more expensive but wallboard has two important advantages. Being plastic-coated, the wallboard will never need painting. For the same reason, wallboard is cleaned very easily because waste materials do not stick to its surface.

Painting and cleaning are the two biggest headaches in bird-room maintenance. Emulsion paint is water-based and, when dry, forms a tough, plastic film. Like any other paint, it needs a surface onto which it can key. The smooth surface of hardboard does not provide such a key and you may find, in extreme conditions, that emulsion paint applied to this surface comes away in large flakes. To overcome this problem, hardboard used for lining should be fixed with the smooth side inwards, leaving the rough side to be painted. This ensures that the emulsion paint gives a good finish, but it does create another problem: the rough surface provides a good key for the paint, but it also provides a good key for droppings. A good, regular scrubbing down will keep the lining clean, but compared with the wipe-down with a damp cloth, which is all that is required for wallboard, I think you will appreciate the labour saved by using wallboard. Of course, if you are intending to keep budgerigars or similar birds, which are inclined to attack the woodwork, you must make sure that there are no areas of wallboard which can be attacked. Your birds will not appreciate a crop full of plastic.

Insulation is a subject which is often in the news with regard to saving fuel. Most bird-rooms require some level of heating and it is obviously to your advantage to reduce heat loss as much as possible. Even if you do not intend to heat the bird-room, you will find that insulation is an advantage as it not only keeps heat in, but also keeps it out. Therefore the temperature inside the bird-room will remain at a much more comfortable level when the weather is hot and sunny, as well as when it is cold.

The only practical, easily obtainable, insulation material is fibre-glass. This is sold in rolls. Remember that, if fibre-glass is compressed, its insulation efficiency is reduced. There is a 2 in (50 mm) gap between the outer cladding and the lining of the module and it is the 2 in (50 mm) thick fibre-glass that should be used.

The insulation material and lining should be fitted when the panel is constructed. Wear gardening or rubber gloves when handling the fibre-glass. Lay the module face downwards and roll the fibre-glass into place. The lining can then be nailed into position, using plated panel pins to avoid staining due to rust. Try to trap the edge of the fibre-glass roll between the framework and the top edge of the lining. This will prevent the insulation working its way down the wall under the force of gravity.

The floor module

Figure 11 shows the end view of the floor module. This is a panel, in this case 6 ft (1.8 m) wide by 6 ft 4 in (1.9 m) long, made from matching supported on 4 × 2 in (100 × 50 mm) bearers, spaced as shown. Particular attention should be paid to the treatment of the floor bearers, as these members are the most liable to rot. Several coats of preservative should be brushed well into the timber.

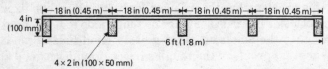

Figure 11 Floor module: end view

The roof module

The arrangement of the roof module is shown in Figure 12. For standardisation and simplicity, all the walls of the bird-room have been designed to the same height. Therefore, the necessary slope to the roof must be provided within the roof module itself. This is achieved by using 4 × 2 in (100 × 50 mm) timber as roof beams and sawing these beams to the shape shown in Figure 12a. It is more economic to cut two beams from one piece of 6 × 2 in (150 × 50 mm), but this size of timber is not always readily available. The roof

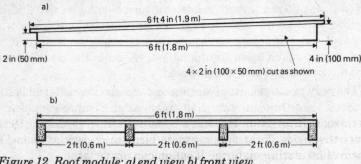

Figure 12 Roof module: a) end view b) front view

module is clad with matching. The modules shown are only suitable for spans of up to 8 ft (2.4 m). Larger spans than this, which are very rarely required, have to be covered by two modules, facing each other to form an apex roof, as shown in Figure 13. This arrangement requires a central support of 6 × 2 in (150 × 50 mm) section, running along the length of the bird-room. The roof modules can be attached to the walls by means of wood screws, but the best method is to use angle brackets. Fascia boards must be provided front and back, to cover the gap at the end of the module, and also large boards at each end. These, and the method of covering the roof, will be described in Chapter 5.

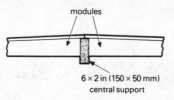

Figure 13 Apex roof for spans or more than 8 ft (2.4 m)

The width of the roof module is dependent upon the layout of the wall modules. For example, if the end modules of your bird-room are 6 ft (1.8 m) wide and fitted between the wall modules, then the out-side dimension of the bird-room, discounting the cladding, will be the width of the end module — which is 6 ft (1.8 m) — plus two frame thicknesses — 4 in (100 mm), making a total of 6 ft 4 in (1.9 mm). This will be the width required for the roof modules. I recommend this method, as the alternative arrangement of the walls and ends requires the provision of one non-standard-length roof module.

Lining and insulation: Insulation must be considered at this stage. It is possible to insulate the roof in the same manner as the walls, i.e. by using fibre-glass mat under a lining panel, fixed across the under-side of the beams. As the lining hangs horizontally, you may find it helpful to provide cross-members between the roof beams to prevent it sagging. An alternative method is to stick insulating tiles to the underside of the matching. This is quite efficient and does give a little more head-room. It is not advisable to fit these tiles to the roof over the inside flight area as some birds may peck at them. Any form of insulating material, if eaten, can prove fatal.

4
Flight module construction

Flight modules

In the discussion of the design parameters for the flight modules (Chapter 2), it was decided that the optimum size, to allow for both adaptability and economy, was 6 × 3 ft (1.8 × 0.9 m). If you wish to economise further on timber then the module width may be increased, but I would not advise going beyond 6 ft (1.8 m). 2 × 2 in (50 × 50 mm) timber is used for the flight wall module framework. Joints are formed according to the previous instructions. The modules are covered with wire netting. This can be the ordinary galvanised wire netting or the welded, square mesh netting, e.g. that sold under the name of 'Twilweld'. The advantage of the latter is that it can be obtained in a much heavier gauge of wire. This not only extends its life, but also makes it easier to fit to the framework. The mesh and gauge of the netting will depend upon the species of bird which you plan to keep, but, unless you intend to specialise in parrot-like birds, I would recommend 1 × ½ in (25 × 12 mm) mesh as a good standard. Netting is sold in various widths, but, for these modules, I have specified 3 ft (0.9 m) wide netting. Netting is usually available in rolls either 19 ft 8 in (6 m) or 39 ft (12 m) long.

Wall module

Figure 14 shows the basic flight wall module. Its construction is simple. The framework is made up of 2 × 2 in (50 × 50 mm) and treated with wood preservative. When the preservative has dried, nail pieces of scrap timber across the corners of the frame to hold it

32

square while the wire netting is fixed in position. The squareness of the framework is most important. When fixing the netting it must be tensioned so that it does not sag in the middle and the scrap timber must be able to withstand this treatment. The netting is secured with staples. With a panel constructed as shown, there should be a cut edge of netting at the top and bottom of the framework. These cut edges should be covered to prevent the birds injuring themselves. The best material for this purpose is the builder's lath. These laths are wooden strips about 1 in (25 mm) wide by ¼ in (6 mm) deep, intended for the repair of the old-fashioned lath and plaster walls. They are also used to construct trellis work, although if you ask for trellis laths you may be sold cedar wood laths which are much more expensive. The laths are cut to size and nailed over the cut edges of the wire, after which they should be treated with preservative.

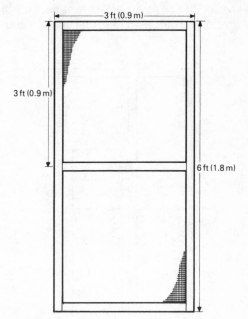

Figure 14 Flight wall module

Although the netting is galvanised it is advisable to paint it with black bitumastic paint. Apply this with a roller, after first applying a metal primer. This process is rather a messy operation and should be carried out with a plastic sheet under the module. In spite of this it is well worthwhile, as not only do you increase the life of the netting, but the matt black finish disguises the netting and makes the birds much easier to see.

Flight door module

This module is illustrated in Figure 15. The door itself is 4 ft 6 in (1.35 m) high by 1 ft 6 in (0.45 m) wide. If the door is hinged so that it opens inwards, and the module positioned so that the door is in the corner of the flight, you should find a safety porch unnecessary, as the birds will find it difficult to fly past a person entering the flight.

The main framework of the module should be constructed first. The door aperture can then be measured and the door frame made to fit the opening. The netting is fixed with staples and laths as before. Do not forget to cover the cut edges. Preservative and bitumastic paint can be applied at the appropriate stages. The door is hung as described and a closing bolt provided on the right-hand side.

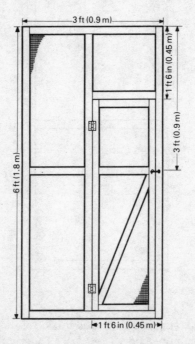

Figure 15 Flight door module

Flight roof module

This module (see Figures 16 and 17) has been designed with the same slope as the bird-room roof. There is no need for a sloping roof if the modules are covered only with netting, except, from the aesthetic point of view, to match the bird-room. However, in most cases you will wish to cover part of the flight roof with translucent PVC roofing sheet and in this case the slope is required to throw off rainwater. The framework is constructed from 4 × 2 in (100 × 50 mm) and 2 × 2 in (50 × 50 mm) timber as shown. The supporting beams can be cut from 4 × 2 in (100 × 50 mm) timber, or, more economically, two beams can be cut from a length of 6 × 2 in (150 × 50 mm). The netting is attached to the top of the framework and all

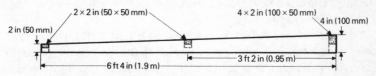

Figure 16 Flight roof module: sectional side view

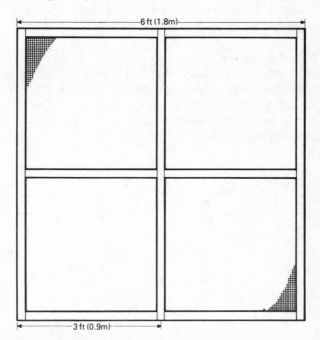

Figure 17 Flight roof module: view from above

edges are covered with laths for added security. If you wish to economise further, the end beams, which will be attached to adjacent roof modules, can be constructed from 4 × 1 in (100 × 25 mm) timber. The overall dimensions of the module must remain the same. The same rules apply to the width of the roof module as to the bird-room roof.

Safety porches

Safety porches are a means of providing a double door at the entrance to the flight, so arranged that the safety porch door may be closed before the flight door is opened. Any birds which escape through the open flight door are thus confined to the safety porch and cannot escape.

I do not believe safety porches to be an absolute necessity, but this, of course, is a matter of personal preference. A permanent safety porch is quite a substantial addition to the flight and can, therefore, add a fair amount to the cost. In addition, safety porches tend to detract from the appearance of the flight, often looking as if they have been added as an afterthought.

Portable safety porch
One useful solution to the problem of safety porches is shown in Figure 18. This is a portable safety porch which can easily be slipped into place over the flight entrance. This piece of equipment is particularly useful in situations where a range of several small aviaries are in use.

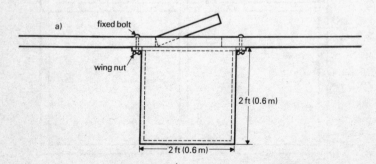

Figure 18 Portable safety porch: a) plan view

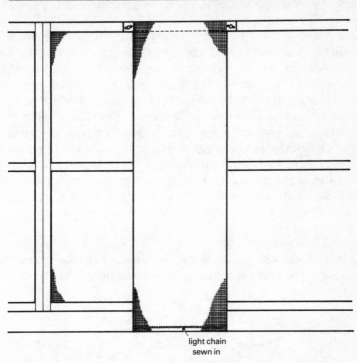

light chain
sewn in

b) front view

The porch consists of a framework, constructed from 2×1 in
(50×25 mm) timber, upon which is hung a curtain of mesh material.
The curtain can be made from any of several different materials,
provided that it is tough and flexible. I would recommend close-
woven net curtaining material. This is made of man-made fibre and,
although it may tear if caught on a sharp projection, it should give
years of service.

This may seem a rather strange choice of material, but there is a
very limited range of readily available materials and it is net curtaining which best meets our requirements. You may think that some
form of plastic garden netting will do the job better, but any netting
used must be of very small mesh — to prevent escaping birds
becoming tangled in the net — and the net itself must hang freely
and not be prone to tangles.

A length of light chain is sewn to the bottom edge of the netting to weight it, so that it hangs in its correct position and is not blown about in the wind.

The framework is made up as shown in Figure 18; the top is covered with a sheet of hardboard. As the safety porch will be stored when not in use, the framework and hardboard can be finished with polyurethane varnish, which will give all the protection required.

Two rustproof bolts, permanently fixed in the flight framework, must be provided above each flight door. The safety porch framework has two corresponding holes through which the bolts will project when the safety porch is in place. The porch is secured by two wing nuts. Provided that the bolts and nuts are kept clean, and given the occasional coating of grease on the threads, the safety porch can be attached or removed in a matter of minutes. The porch is very effective for its purpose except on very windy days.

Fixed safety porch
Figure 19 shows a typical arrangement, suitable for a flight constructed from the standard modules described. The two sides are

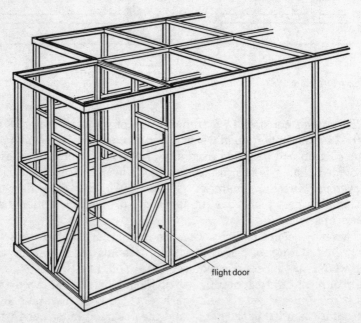

flight door

Figure 19 Fixed safety porch

standard 3 ft (0.9 m) wall modules, while the end is a door module as shown in Figure 15. The door should open outwards and should have a catch on the inside as well as the outside. The roof module, shown in Figure 20, is a scaled-down version of the standard flight roof module. The safety porch is attached to the end of the flight, around the door. The foundations of the flight must, of course, be extended to cater for the safety porch.

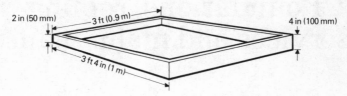

Figure 20 Safety porch roof

5

Foundations, roofing, services and maintenance

Foundations

If the aviary is to provide good service then it must be based on good foundations. The extent of these foundations depends upon the sub-soil. On clay, for example, the foundations have to withstand the considerable expansion and contraction of the sub-soil, according to the amount of water present. However, the foundations described in this chapter should prove adequate on any sub-soil for an average-sized prefabricated wooden bird-room, i.e. up to 20×10 ft (6 × 3 m).

Figure 21 shows foundations suitable for a bird-room with a wooden floor. The floor joists are supported at 3 ft (0.9 m) intervals.

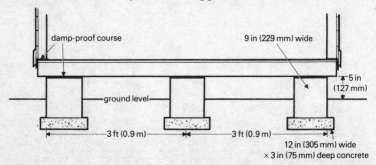

Figure 21 Bird-room foundations: for a wooden floor

The floor of the bird-room should be at least 5 in (127 mm) above ground level in order to prevent water splashing up onto the wood-work. To construct the foundations, trenches should be excavated down to the firm sub-soil. In the example shown, three trenches are required. The bases of the foundations are three concrete slabs, 12 in (305 mm) wide by 3 in (75 mm) deep, ideally running the full length of the bird-room. Concrete can be laid to form these slabs or paving slabs can be used. Paving slabs are not 3 in (75 mm) thick but they are quite adequate. A 9 in (229 mm) wide pier or wall is built up on each concrete base to the required height. These can be constructed from bricks or concrete blocks. The latter are by far the simplest to use.

Before placing the floor in position, a damp-proof course should be provided between the floor and the foundations. This can be either proper damp-proof course material or plastic sheet. The purpose of this membrane is to prevent damp rising in the floor joists. A wooden floor must be well ventilated to prevent rot and the foundations should be sited so that there is no obstruction to the flow of air under the floor.

Should you wish to provide a concrete floor for your bird-room then the arrangement shown in Figure 22 should be used. An area equivalent to that of the entire bird-room must be excavated to a sufficient depth to give the required 5 in (127 mm) clearance between ground level and the bottom of the bird room. If the site for the bird-room is flat, a depth of 12 in (305 mm) will be sufficient. If the site is sloping, then one side will need to be excavated to a greater depth to allow the floor to be horizontal. Remember that in no place should the floor level be less than 5 in (127 mm) above ground level.

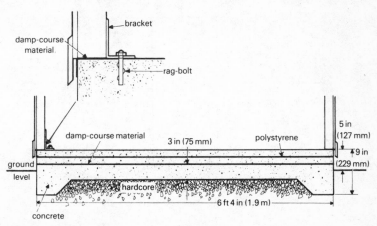

Figure 22 Bird-room foundations: for a concrete floor

The concrete floor is laid on a bed of hardcore 6 in (150 mm) thick. The edges can be arranged to give a greater depth of concrete, as shown in the illustration, but this is not essential and the floor can be laid as a flat raft of concrete. A plastic damp-proof course sheet is essential to prevent water rising through the concrete and there should be 3 in (75 mm) of concrete under this sheet. Concrete floors can be very cold in winter and, to provide insulation, a layer of poly-styrene, up to ½ in (12 mm) thick can be laid above the damp-proof course. It may be possible to obtain polystyrene of this thickness, but most do-it-yourself shops sell rolls of this material about ⅛ in (3 mm) thick and several layers of this will do very well. With this type of floor, it is practical to insert rag-bolts into the concrete to provide an attachment for the walls of the bird-room.

You should bear in mind that a concrete floor does place limi-tations of the flexibility of your aviary. Any future re-arrangement of the layout could involve breaking up and disposing of a large quantity of concrete. The foundations required for a wooden floor are easily demolished and the materials can be used again.

The foundations for the flight need not be as strong as those for the bird-room. They have much less weight to carry. They do, how-ever, serve a dual purpose, having to be both functional and decorative. The suggested arrangement is shown in Figure 23. This is a scaled-down version of the bird-room foundations. The wall or pier can be constructed from either ornamental bricks or concrete

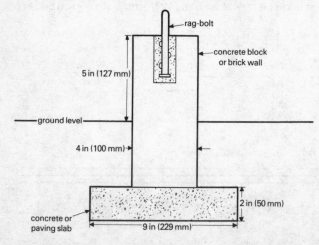

Figure 23 Flight foundations

blocks. The latter can be painted with a textured exterior wall finish to give them a more attractive appearance. A good-quality emulsion paint is an acceptable alternative, although it may not last as long. Rag-bolts can be grouted into the wall to hold down the flight.

The most valuable piece of equipment used in the construction of foundations is the spirit level. It is absolutely essential that the foundations are level, particularly in the case of the flights. Any inaccuracies in the level of the bird-room foundations can be adjusted by placing pieces of wood of a suitable thickness between the floor joists and the damp-proof course material. This process can be adopted for the flight, any gaps appearing as a result of the adjustment can be filled with mortar.

Roof

Construction
The construction of the roof modules is described in Chapter 3. The roof is fixed to the walls by means of angle brackets, as shown in Figure 24. When the roof is in position you will see that additional lengths of timber need to be fitted in order to finish off the roof. A piece of timber, known as a barge board, is usually fitted at each end of the roof. This is mostly decorative in purpose and can be omitted if desired. Further lengths of timber should be fitted along the front and back of the roof to close the gaps between beams. These are known as fascia boards. A board to support the guttering, as shown in Figure 24, is a useful addition. Although the area under the eaves is covered by hardboard, it is preferable to cover it with timber of a similar thickness to the fascia boards. This not only improves the finish, but protects the roof against splashes from the gutter. Note that the fascia and eaves boards are fitted before the roofing felt and the barge boards are fitted last of all. All the timber should be treated with preservative in the same manner as the rest of the bird-room modules.

Covering
The roof should be covered with roofing felt. There are several grades of felt available, but I would recommend green, sand-faced felt. This is heavy gauge and has a sanded surface which improves its appearance and extends its life. All felt has a tendency to crack if handled without care. If you can lay the felt on a warm day you will find the process easier, as the felt is more flexible when warm.

Frosty days are to be avoided. The felt should be laid from the lower part of the roof upwards, so that the upper layers overlap the lower, thus providing a waterproof joint. Use a roofing compound to stick the felt to the roof and fasten it into place with aluminium felt tacks.

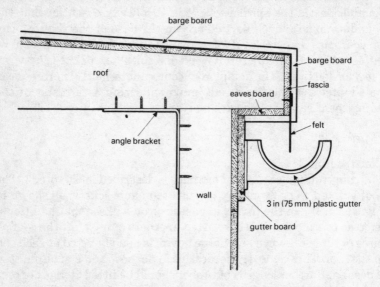

Figure 24 Roofing and guttering

As shown in Figure 24, the lower edge of the felt should hang down into the gutter so that rainwater will drip off without running back under the eaves.

Guttering and drainage

It is always advisable to provide guttering on the bird-room. Without guttering, the rainwater will run down the back of the structure and damp will soon penetrate the walls and eventually cause rot. 3 in (75 mm) plastic guttering is sufficient for the average bird-room and is readily available.

The rainwater must be disposed of in some way, e.g. by a water butt, soakaway or via an existing surface water drain. A water butt is recommended as it requires little effort to connect to the drainage system and the collected rainwater is useful in the garden.

Bird-room services

Services is a general term used to cover the requirements of an establishment in regard to ventilation, heating, lighting and electrical supplies.

Ventilation is essential in a bird-room, particularly in the case of a canary bird-room, where the birds live in cages without access to outside flights. Bird-rooms must be dry and warm, but a constant flow of fresh air, without draughts, is essential to the health of your birds. Hot, stale air rises and so a ventilator is needed at a high point to allow this air to escape. Further ventilators can be positioned at the bottom of the wall to allow the inflow of fresh air. The slotted or louvred type of ventilator is best suited to this arrangement, preferably one which can be closed when required. At the other end of the scale is the thermostatically controlled extractor fan. These fans should only be considered for the larger bird-room, as they tend to be too powerful for the average establishment. In most bird-rooms the ventilation can be further improved in hot weather by providing opening windows.

Heating, like lighting, is a subject around which arguments have raged for many years. Many of the senior members of the canary fancy will not allow heating or lighting in their bird-rooms at any price, blaming these artificial aids for many problems, ranging from infertility to soft moult. However, if you are a foreign-bird enthusiast they are essential aids. I believe that a certain amount of heating is beneficial not only to the birds, but also to the bird-keeper. It is certainly no pleasure to attend to your birds' needs on a winter's night in sub-zero temperatures. I am not suggesting that a high level of temperature is maintained; 40°F (5°C) is quite sufficient. If a higher temperature is required, for example to acclimatise foreign birds, this can be provided locally.

There is only one economic and safe way to provide heating in the bird-room and that is with thermostatically controlled electric heaters. The alternative is to use a paraffin or Calor gas heater. These heaters cannot be controlled. Once set they continue to give out the same amount of heat and this means that the bird-room can become either too hot or too cold. Another important disadvantage is that both paraffin and Calor gas give off large quantities of water when burning. While a reasonable level of humidity is essential in the bird-room during the breeding season, the level of humidity reached when using these heaters is excessive and causes unhealthy, damp conditions.

A thermostatically controlled electric heater will maintain a constant level of heat in your bird-room to within a few degrees. The best type is the sealed tubular heater sold for horticultural purposes. This is absolutely safe and will provide for many years of service. The size of heater will depend on a number of factors: the volume of the bird-room, the amount of insulation provided, the geographical location and the level of heat required. It is best to use a powerful heater. This uses no more power than a lower wattage heater, as it will heat up the bird-room more quickly and be on for less time. As a guide, a 2 kW heater is adequate for the 10 × 6 ft (3 × 1.8 m) bird-room previously described. The tubular heaters recommended can be placed in strategic positions around the bird-room, e.g. under the windows. The thermostat must be placed in a position where it will give an accurate control of temperature. You may find it necessary to experiment with the thermostat settings. As hot air rises, you will find that the top tier of cages in the bird-room will be warmer than that at the bottom. This situation is inevitable and the thermostat should be set to give the correct temperature at the lower levels. The two or three degrees extra warmth at the upper levels is an unavoidable bonus for the birds in these cages.

Other types of electric heater available are convector, radiant and fan heaters. The convector heater is quite useful, but care must be taken to see that seed husks or water do not get in, a difficult task, as the top and bottom of the heater must be open to allow it to operate. Radiant electric heaters of the bar type should never be used because of the fire danger. Infra-red heaters, which are also radiant heaters, are useful in some instances to provide local heat, but limit them to the small, lamp-like heaters used in chick-brooders. Fan heaters can be used to provide quick heat but they do tend to be noisy and are not really intended for use in a bird-room environment.

In spite of many arguments to the contrary, I believe lighting to be essential in the bird-room. There are few bird-keepers who can arrive home early enough in the winter months to be able to attend to their birds' needs during daylight hours. The level of lighting should not be high, as the birds may be brought into breeding condition at the wrong time. A time switch to control the lighting is a very useful piece of equipment. With this control you can be sure that the lighting will go on and off at pre-set times in your absence.

A further refinement is to use a dimmer, which allows the lighting to come on or go off gradually. This will help to ensure that the birds will go to roost in a natural manner. A sudden switching off of lighting tends to frighten birds and may cause them to flutter around the flight or cage. Note that fluorescent light cannot be controlled by a dimmer. A suitable alternative to a dimmer is a night-light. This can be a 15 W lamp, wired in isolation from the time switch so that it remains on all the time. The level of light from a lamp of this size is sufficient to allow the birds to find a roosting spot or return to their nests, but not high enough for them to remain active. Running costs are negligible in comparison with its usefulness.

The use of electric heating and lighting in the bird-room presumes that there is an electricity supply available and, more particularly, raises the question of the wiring of the bird-room. This is not a task for the uninitiated to tackle, due to the inherent dangers. Ask a qualified electrician to do the job for you, or at least to direct the work. You can then be sure that there will be no hidden dangers in your bird-room.

Erection and maintenance

The erection of aviaries is not difficult, providing a few, simple rules are observed. The prime requirement is a level base. This should be easily achieved if the foundations are laid properly (see page 40).

The bird-room should be assembled first. Lay the wooden floor in position and check that it is level in all directions by means of a spirit level. If there are any inaccuracies, packing pieces, in the form of scrap timber, can be used to correct the level. Assemble two corner modules, check that the walls are vertical and work from this datum. Provided that the foundations are level and the walls vertical, there should be no difficulty in assembling the rest of the bird-room. Attaching and covering the roof and the guttering and drainage arrangement have been described already. The barge boards should have a strip of mastic inserted between their inside faces and the roof to prevent water running down the gap and causing rot.

Figures 21 and 22 show the bird-room foundations. The bottom of the wall modules is also shown. The shaped piece of timber shown on the outside of the wall, overlapping the floor, is a useful addition which encourages rainwater to drip away from the bottom of the walls. This also should be sealed with mastic.

Damp-proof material should be laid between the floor and the walls of the bird-room. The walls can be fixed to the floor with wood screws where there is a wooden floor. With a concrete floor, angle brackets should be screwed to the bird-room walls to provide an attachment to the rag-bolts grouted into the concrete (see Figure 22, enlarged view).

There is little to add in describing the erection of the flight. The modules are best joined by means of wood screws as this gives a better finish than coach-bolts. Do not tighten down the nuts on the rag bolts (see Figure 23) until the flight is completely assembled. This will give scope for any adjustment required. A finishing touch to the flight is to fix a length of 4 in (100 mm) wide timber around the top of the flight to hide the join between roof and walls. This is entirely aesthetic and does improve the appearance of the flight.

There is little point in taking care over the construction and erection of your aviary if you neglect its maintenance. A regular programme of maintenance, preferably during late autumn, will add years to the life of your establishment and can prevent the loss of birds.

The wire netting of the flight is the most vulnerable part of the aviary. The netting needs close inspection every year, particularly if the flight is planted and the shrubbery comes near the netting. Rust can set in very quickly and sections of netting can quite literally disintegrate. Frequently the first indication of this is when you see your birds flying around the garden! The wire netting should be inspected regularly and any suspect areas replaced. An annual coat of bitumastic paint is a must.

Bird-room woodwork should also be given an annual treatment with wood preservative. The roofing felt should be inspected for any tears or loose sections which might be weak points in winter gales. Hinges and door bolts can be oiled and a last, but important, point is to check any electrical installations.

Most maintenance is a matter of commonsense, but it is often neglected. A few hours spent each year on repairs can save a great deal of expense in the future.

6
Cages

Cages are an essential part of aviary equipment, no matter which branch of the hobby you pursue. Breeding cages are essential for the controlled production of exhibition birds. Flight cages are required to house birds outside the breeding season, when access to flights, for some reason, is not available. Breeding cages can be converted into flight cages if removable slides are fitted. These cages may be constructed in a number of ways. The traditional method is the box cage, which, as its name implies, is basically an open wooden box, the open side being covered with a wire cage front. This type of cage has proved extremely successful over the last one hundred years. However, it is also the most expensive, although it does present the most flexible arrangement possible.

The alternative to the box cage is to build cages as an integral part of your bird-room, rather like shelves. The bird-room must be lined for this method, as the lining will act as the back and sides of the cages. This system allows you to make maximum use of the available space and is, of course, far more economic in terms of materials used. You should bear in mind that what you gain in economy, you lose in flexibility, although, if your layout has been planned with forethought, this should present no problems.

Shelf-type breeding cages

Figure 25 shows the simplest method of constructing built-in breeding cages. For want of a better name I have described them as 'shelf-type' cages. ½ in (12 mm) plywood or blockboard is used for

49

the shelves, each of which forms not only the floor of a cage but also the roof of the one below it. The shelves are cut 12 in (305 mm) wide to the required length. Battens of 1 × 1 in (25 × 25 mm) timber are screwed to the walls of the bird-room at 15 in (380 mm) intervals. The shelves are then dropped into place on these supporting battens and fastened with wood screws. ¼ × ¼ in (6 × 6 mm) strip is glued and pinned in place as shown to form the guides for the partitions or slides between the cages.

The front rail is cut from a piece of ½ in (12 mm) plywood. This should be 2½ in (63 mm) wide and as long as required for the size of cage. A strip ¾ in (18 mm) wide is cut from the front rail (see Figure 25) to provide a means of cleaning-out the cage. This is secured by means of two U-shaped hooks which pass through the cut-out. These can be made from heavy gauge wire. A length of wire from an old cage front is ideal.

The ends of two 2 in (50 mm) wire nails are filed flat and the two nails inserted into holes drilled in the cage floor as shown. The nails can be glued in position. Holes must then be drilled in the front rail, so that the rail may fit over and be held in position by the two nails. The cage front can then be sprung into place, the spikes on the top and bottom of the cage front fitting into holes drilled at appropriate positions in the roof and front rail. The partitions can be constructed from hardboard or a wire slide can be used.

This simple form of cage construction may seem rather crude, but it is effective and also has the great advantage that the cages can be taken down in a few minutes, thus making cleaning and renovation an easy task. No cleaning tray is provided.

Framed breeding cages

For those who prefer a more substantial arrangement, with a cleaning tray, the layout shown in Figure 26 should meet their requirements. I have used the term 'framed' breeding cages to distinguish them from the previous example and because they have a timber framework which supports the front of the cages. As before, the floor and roof of each cage is formed from ½ in (12 mm) plywood supported on 1 × 1 in (25 × 25 mm) battens screwed to the walls of the bird-room. The recommended depth of the cage is 12 in (305 mm); the length ('L') again depends upon the space available for cages.

The fronts of the cages are supported by vertical members cut

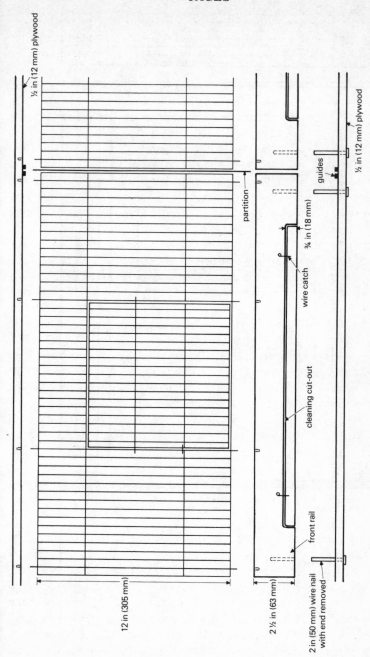

Figure 25 Shelf-type breeding cage

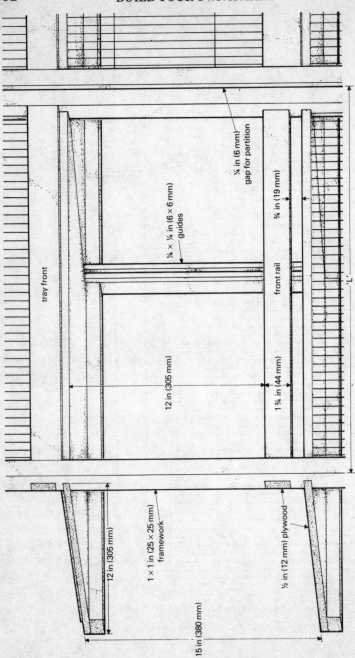

¼ in (6 mm)
gap for partition

¾ in (19 mm)

¼ × ¼ in (6 × 6 mm)
guides

tray front

front rail

12 in (305 mm)

1 ¾ in (44 mm)

12 in (305 mm)

1 × 1 in (25 × 25 mm)
framework

½ in (12 mm) plywood

15 in (380 mm)

Figure 26 Framed breeding cage

from 1 × 1 in (25 × 25 mm) timber, to the dimensions shown in Figure 27. Two cage tiers are shown and more can be provided by repeating the group of cut-outs.

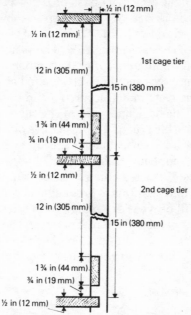

Figure 27 Framed breeding cage: vertical support

Having fixed the cage floors in position, the vertical supports are screwed in place. Reference to Figure 26 will show the arrangement. Note that a ¼ in (6 mm) gap must be left between the vertical supports to allow the slide to be inserted.

Screw a length of 1 × 1 in (25 × 25 mm) timber in a position opposite to the gap between the supports. Glue and pin two lengths of ¼ × ¼ in (6 × 6 mm) timber to the top of this section, ¼ in (6 mm) apart, to form a guide to hold the slide in position. This is a better arrangement than horizontal guides, as the latter tend to become filled up with seed and husks. Next cut a front rail for each cage from ½ in (12 mm) plywood. This should be 1¾ in (44 mm) wide, the length being the same as the distance between the outside faces of the two vertical supports (dimension 'L' in Figure 26). Screw the front rail into position.

The cage front is sprung into position as described for the shelf-type cages.

The tray (Figure 28) is purposely designed in a simple manner. The front is a piece of ½ in (12 mm) plywood, 2½ in (63 mm) wide. Its length is the distance between the inside faces of the vertical supports less ⅛ in (3 mm). The base of the tray is cut from hardboard and should be 12½ in (317 mm) deep as shown. The hardboard is pinned and glued to the front. This type of tray leaves a narrow strip at each end of the cage uncovered. This is not important and to alter the situation would unnecessarily complicate the design.

The finish of the cages should be considered at this point. All the timber used in the cage manufacture should be well rubbed-down with glasspaper. The back and sides of the cages are formed by the existing walls of the bird-room. If the lining is plastic-faced plywood, there is no further work to be done. If the lining is hardboard, it can be painted with emulsion paint or finished with polyurethane varnish. The base of the tray should be sealed with polyurethane varnish. You will find that this is proof against most forms of cleaning agents and will prevent droppings from sticking to the base. I would not advise the use of enamel paint on the cages as it takes some time to dry and gives off fumes in the process. This may not be important initially, but when you come to repaint the cages it could cause problems.

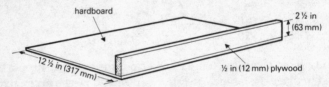

Figure 28 Framed breeding cage: tray

Box-type cages

Figure 29 shows a typical double box-type breeding cage. This cage can also be built as a treble or in blocks of cages. In my opinion to build one of these cages larger than a double-breeder cancels out their advantage, which is flexibility. The double-breeder can be moved around with ease; anything larger is difficult to handle.

The sides, top and bottom of the cage are constructed from ⅜ in (9 mm) plywood. In the example described, the sides measure 15¼ × 12 in (386 × 305 mm) and the top and bottom are each 12 in (305 mm) wide by the required length. The sections are glued and pinned together and all joints are filled with adhesive so that there

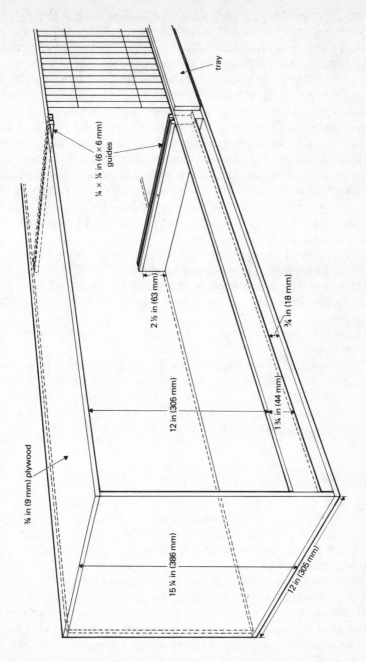

tray

¼ × ¼ in (6 × 6 mm) guides

2 ½ in (63 mm)

¾ in (18 mm)

1 ¾ in (44 mm)

12 in (305 mm)

⅜ in (9 mm) plywood

15 ¼ in (386 mm)

12 in (305 mm)

Figure 29 Double box-type breeding cage

are no potential hiding places for vermin. The back of the cage can also be cut from plywood but hardboard will do just as well. A bottom guide is provided both to act as a guide for the sliding partition and to stiffen up the structure of the cage. Its base needs to be ¾ in (18 mm) thick. This thickness is achieved by glueing together two pieces of ⅜ in (9 mm) plywood. It is cut to 2½ × 12 in (63 × 305 mm), with a recess at one end to fit around the front rail (see Figure 29). Two 12 in (305 mm) lengths of ¼ × ¼ in (6 × 6 mm) timber are glued and pinned ¼ in (6 mm) apart on top of the base to provide the actual guides. Two more pieces of ¼ × ¼ in (6 mm) timber are positioned at the top of the cage to provide the top guides. The front rail is made from a strip of ⅜ in (9 mm) plywood, 1¾ in (44 mm) wide and as long as the internal dimension of the cage. This is glued and pinned into place ¾ in (18 mm) above the floor of the cage.

The tray is shown in Figure 28. This takes the same form as the previous examples, i.e. a sheet of hardboard 12½ in (317 mm) deep with a ½ in (12 mm) plywood front 2½ in (63 mm) deep. This type of tray is very efficient and, being inexpensive, can be renewed when required.

The cage front is sprung into position, the spikes fitting into pre-drilled holes.

The cages can be finished in emulsion paint or, in this case, a lead-free gloss paint. The latter can be used as the cages can be removed from the bird-room for re-painting. Gloss paint does give a better finish and one which is easier to clean. The tray should be sealed with polyurethane varnish.

Perches

The final requirement in cage construction is the provision of perches. These are usually constructed from hardwood dowel, the diameter of which is chosen to suit the variety of bird. In some cases a square perch is recommended rather than round, particularly for some varieties of canaries.

Dowel is convenient to use and easy to clean. However, it is rather rigid and some species of bird may get foot trouble from its unyielding nature. To overcome this problem the perches can be fixed as shown in Figure 30. A rectangular piece of wood is cut to shape so that it can be attached to the perch and pushed between two of the cage front wires. By rotating the end through 90° it is held between the cage front wires. The other end of the perch is not supported. When the bird lands on the perch, the springiness of the wire allows the perch to give; the action approximates to that of a natural branch and reduces the shock to the birds' feet.

Natural twigs may be used as perches for foreign birds, but these may not be available to the town dweller.

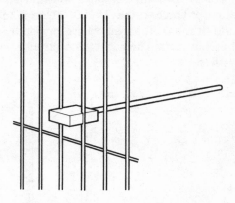

Figure 30 Perching

Hospital cage

The hospital cage is an essential item of equipment for any bird-keeper. On the rare occasion when a bird falls ill, the best treatment readily available is to place it in a warm atmosphere. The hospital cage provides just such a controlled environment. It is possible to refine its design to provide such luxuries as thermostatically controlled heat, but the emphasis of this book is on simplicity and the hospital cage described will be found to be efficient in most circumstances.

Figure 31 shows the arrangement of the hospital cage. It is a box-type cage; part of the front is covered with a sheet of glass and heat is provided by a 25 W or 40 W lamp, situated in the lower section. A glass front is provided, rather than the usual wire front, in order to conserve heat. The cage is constructed from ¼ in (6 mm) plywood. Cut four sections; one 11½ × 5¼ in (291 × 133 mm) for the roof, one 11½ × 6 in (291 × 150 mm) for the base and two 15 × 6 in (380 ×

150 mm) for the sides. The top and bottom are fitted between the sides to give a finished outside dimension of 15 × 12 in (380 × 305 mm). The right-hand side of the cage has an access door. This is in the style of the show-cage door. A 4 in (100 mm) square is cut out of the side. This is hinged at the top, using ¾ in (18 mm) brass hinges, and a U-shaped catch, constructed from heavy gauge wire, is provided at the bottom. The top should have two sets of four ¼ in (6 mm) diameter holes drilled in it, to act as ventilation holes.

The dimensions of the back are 14½ × 11½ in (367 × 291 mm). The back should fit inside the framework formed by the sides, top and bottom, to make a rigid box. All the sections should be pinned and glued together.

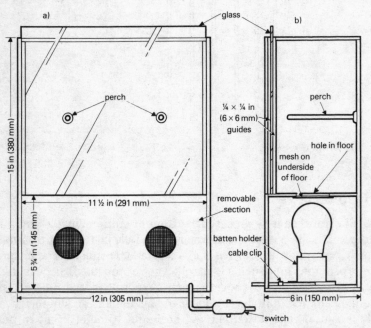

Figure 31 Hospital cage: a) front view b) end view (side removed)

Next cut a piece of plywood 11½ × 5½ in (291 × 139 mm) to form the floor. Cut a 2½ in (63 mm) square hole out of the centre to allow the heat from the lamp to rise into the cage. A piece of perforated zinc sheet or expanded aluminium mesh should be fixed under the hole. This allows the heat to rise into the top section but prevents the bird from gaining access to the lamp. The floor is fixed into position so that the top of the floor is 5¾ in (145 mm) above the top face of the base. Two strips of ¼ × ¼ in (6 × 6 mm) should then be fitted to either side of the cage front to act as guides for the glass. The guides must be positioned so that the glass rests on the cage floor. If the front edge of the outer guide is flush with the front edge of the floor there should be no problem. The guides should have a minimum gap of ⅛ in (3 mm) between them. You will see that the depth of the roof allows for a slight gap between its edge and the face of the glass. This is to facilitate the insertion and removal of the glass front, but also provides extra ventilation. A sick bird needs to be kept warm, but fresh air is essential.

The lamp is held in a batten holder which stands on what might be termed a drawer. This arrangement is for ease of maintenance. If the lamp needs replacing or cleaning, it is a simple matter to undo two screws and withdraw the lamp assembly.

The lamp assembly is constructed from two pieces of plywood. The front section is 11½ × 5¾ in (291 × 145 mm) Two holes are cut into this section to allow fresh air to enter. These can be 2 in (50 mm) diameter or 2 in (50 mm) square; the circular hole is more pleasing in appearance. The holes should be covered on the inside with the same material used for covering the hole above the lamp. The base of the lamp assembly is 11½ × 5½ in (291 × 139 mm). This is glued and pinned to the front. A hole of suitable diameter should be drilled in the front of the assembly to provide access for the electric cable.

The final task, at this stage, is either to drill a keyhole slot in the back of the cage, so that the cage may be hung on a round-headed screw, or to provide mirror plates to perform the same function.

The whole cage should now be well rubbed down with glasspaper. As this is a hospital cage, cleanliness is important and this can only be achieved with an easily cleaned surface. Give the cage a coat of primer, undercoat and finish off with two coats of lead-free gloss enamel paint. Once this has dried, the lamp can be fitted. Pass the cable through the hole in the front of the lamp assembly, wire up the batten holder and screw it into place. Although the cage is wooden, it is best to use three-core cable and provide an earth. The cable should be tightly held in position by means of a cable clamp. A switch should be provided in the cable itself and the cord should be terminated on a three-pin plug, preferably fused with a 3-amp fuse. The size of the lamp depends upon local conditions. Try a 25 W lamp at first, changing it to a 40 W if required. It should not be necessary, nor is it desirable, to go above this level. The mushroom-type of lamp is best suited to the purpose.

Show-cage-type perches can be fitted or lengths of dowel will serve just as well.

The glass front should measure $11\frac{3}{8} \times 9\frac{1}{2}$ in (288 $\times$ 241 mm) but the width should be checked against the cage when it has been constructed. The extra height on the glass panel allows it to project above the cage top so that it can be gripped by the fingers for removal. If you are concerned about the sharp edges, ask your glass merchant to polish them.

This completes the construction of the cage. When the cage is in use, the temperature inside can be varied by altering the position of the cage in the bird-room and the power of the lamp used. Obviously if you site the hospital cage above a heater, the temperature inside the cage will rise. It is a matter of trial and error to find the best position for the cage, but it is effort that is repaid if you can save a valuable bird.

Food can be provided in small containers stood on the cage floor. Water is best provided in a fountain-type container screwed to the cage wall.

7
Accessories

The aviary, when built, will require a number of accessories before you can consider installing any birds. The more obvious of these are containers for food and water, but you will also need such things as seed bins and, ultimately, nest boxes. Many of these items are available from the trade and it is generally more economical to buy them than make them yourself. Two exceptions to this rule are seed hoppers and nest boxes.

Food containers

Food containers need to be durable, easily cleaned and resistant to being tipped over. Food for softbills can be provided in plastic or glass pots. Seed eaters need a wider range of containers.

In a flight or breeding cage, seed can be provided in the plastic, jam-jar type of hopper. In this hopper, a jam-jar is used to hold the seed which then flows into a plastic base. These hoppers are inexpensive, easy to clean and are virtually indestructible. They will, of course, only accept the smaller seed, such as canary seed and millet. Seed for the larger seed eaters, such as parrots, should be provided in open metal containers which are proof against powerful bills. Canary seed containers are usually small plastic devices hung on the outside of the cage front, a hole being provided through which the canary puts its head to reach the seed.

Aviary seed hopper
In an aviary or flight containing a large number of birds the best way to provide seed is by means of a large seed hopper. These can be

purchased through the trade, but are very expensive. It is not difficult to make a hopper from plywood and a typical arrangement is
shown in Figure 32.

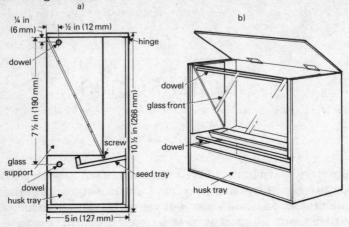

Figure 32 Aviary seed hopper: a) end view (side removed) b) front view

The hopper is constructed from ¼ in (6 mm) plywood; a 2 ft 6 in ×
2 ft (0.75 × 0.6 m) sheet is sufficient to provide all the material
required. As the illustration shows, the seed hopper consists of a
glass-fronted seed container with a removable husk tray beneath. It
is designed for the smaller seed eaters and is not entirely suitable for
budgerigars which tend to destroy wooden equipment very quickly.

To construct the seed hopper, first carefully mark out the following sections on the plywood, making sure that the corners are
square: one back 11¼ × 10 in (291 × 254 mm), two sides 10 × 5 in
(254 × 127 mm), one base 12 × 5 in (305 × 127 mm), one lid 12 ×
5 in (305 × 127 mm), a seed tray base 11½ × 3 in (291 × 75 mm),
seed tray front 11½ × ¾ in (291 × 18 mm), two glass supports 7 ×
3 in (178 × 75 mm), one husk tray base 11⅜ × 4¾ in (288 × 118
mm), one each husk tray front and back 11⅜ × ¾ in (288 × 44 mm)
and two husk tray sides 4¼ × 1¾ in (106 × 44 mm).

Cut the sections carefully and glass paper them smooth. Next
take the two glass support sections and cut them in half diagonally.
Smooth the cut edges, Reference to Figure 32 will show you the
function of these sections.

Taking one side section, fix one half of the glass support in
position with its edge against the front edge of the side. Use
adhesive and panel pins to join the two together.

The other half of the support is then fixed to the side, leaving ⅛ in (3 mm) gap between the two halves. The slot thus formed takes the glass front.

Insert a small round-headed wood screw at the bottom of the slot, as shown, in order to stop the glass in the right position. Repeat this procedure for the other side, remembering that the two sides are mirror images of each other. Now mark out and drill the two ¼ in (6 mm) holes in each side to take the dowel.

Next pin and glue the front of the seed tray to the base. Make sure that the front is well smoothed down with glass paper before assembly. One side can now be fixed in position to the side and back. Note that the correct position of the seed tray is with the upper surface of the rear of the base in line with the bottom of the glass support and the top edge of the front just touching it. The other side should then be attached.

Fix the base in position and put the assembly to one side for the adhesive to set. In the meantime the husk tray can be assembled. This is a simple process and is best started by attaching the front and back to the base.

To make the lid, first screw on the hinges as shown and try the lid on the hopper. Depending upon the type of hinges used, you may find it necessary to recess the back a little to take the hinges so that the lid sits properly. When a satisfactory fit is achieved, screw the hinges to the back.

The two lengths of dowel are fitted next. The purpose of the dowel next to the seed tray is to provide a perch. The dowel at the top of the hopper is there to provide a simple yet effective means of holding together the sides of the hopper.

If this dowel, or something like it, is omitted, then there is a tendency for the weight of the seed to push the sides of the hopper apart, and this might result in the glass front falling out. This dowel should be a tight fit in the holes provided and only a spot of glue should be needed to hold it in position.

Having completed the construction of the hopper, the size of the glass front can now be determined. The width at the top and at the bottom, and the depth should be carefully measured. Obtain a piece of 'picture' glass, the dimensions of which should be ⅛ in (3 mm) less than the size of the aperture.

All that remains is to give the hopper a final rub down with fine glass paper and then apply two coats of polyurethane varnish. You should then have an inexpensive, yet invaluable, addition to your aviary equipment.

Seed bins

It is much cheaper to buy seed in bulk, but this does present a storage problem. Seed is best stored in metal vermin-proof containers. Metal dustbins are ideal, but may be rather large to keep in the average bird-room. Plastic containers are an adequate alternative, but they are not mouse-proof, a fact which should be remembered if the seed is stored separately from the bird-room, which, ideally, should be free from vermin. The plastic bins sold for wine-making are useful. Large ice-cream containers, of the type used by frozen food suppliers, are worth keeping, to store both seed and utensils.

Water containers

In the aviary, water can be supplied in plastic jam-jar hoppers. These must be positioned so that they do not become fouled with seed or droppings. Tubular plastic fountain-type holders can be employed in the breeding or flight cage. These have a slender base which is inserted through the bars of the cage front from the outside. They can be fixed next to a perch above floor level and will, therefore, usually remain clean. Water for canaries is usually supplied in containers hung on the outside of the cage front, in a similar fashion to the seed container.

Nest boxes

Many varieties of birds nest in boxes. These are easily constructed and some typical examples are shown in Figures 33—35. The two cube-shaped boxes are suitable for finches and the oblong box is suitable for budgerigars. The boxes can be made from plywood or timber. If they are intended for an outside flight then an exterior grade of plywood should be used. A removable or openable lid or side is essential. Two methods of providing this facility are shown: the removable section may either run in grooves or be hinged. The size of the box depends upon the species of bird, but the budgerigar nest box must be made to fit the concave block required for these birds. Access to the nest box may be via a hole or a half open front, depending on the species of bird using the box. In all cases, finish the boxes with two coats of polyurethane varnish. This not only protects the wood and makes cleaning easier, but also seals the joints and reduces the possibility of pests taking up residence.

Other species, of course, may require different types of nesting facilities. Canaries, for instance, require plastic nest pans and wax-bills need wicker nesting baskets. These items are best purchased from the trade.

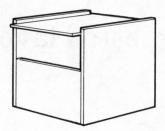

Figure 33 Nest box with sliding top and half open front

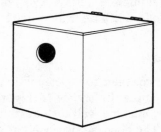

Figure 34 Nest box with hinged top and entrance hole

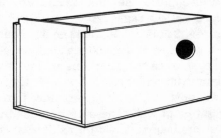

Figure 35 Nest box for budgerigars with sliding door and entrance hole

8
Suggested layouts

In this chapter a number of suggested bird-room and aviary layouts are put forward to illustrate the basic requirements and show what can be done with a minimum outlay. The examples will not suit everyone but they do form a base from which to work.

Canary bird-room

I have taken what I consider to be the minimum practical size of bird-room as an example. Reference to Figure 36 will show the layout of the bird-room. One wall includes four windows, two of which are opening. The door is positioned at the end of the bird-room, although this could be moved to the front wall if required. 3 ft (0.9 m) long by 1 ft (0.3 m) wide double breeding cages are arranged along the back wall, opposite the windows and also along part of the wall opposite the door. The cages can be mounted on a base framework made from 2 × 2 in (50 × 50 mm) timber. Four tiers of cages may be provided, giving a total of sixteen double breeders or thirty-two individual cages when the partitions are inserted. This should give ample accommodation for at least six breeding pairs and their offspring. You will see that shelves are provided next to the bank of cages on the right-hand wall. These are intended to house show cages when birds are being trained for exhibition. These could be replaced by a further bank of breeding cages. A 9 in (229 mm) wide worktop is shown running the length of the wall under the windows. This is a very useful facility when it comes to preparing soft foods or to changing seed and water. Storage space is available under the cages, although the amount of space available is limited and bulk supplies of seed may have to be stored separately from the bird-room.

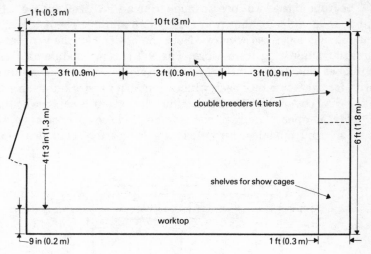

Figure 36 Canary bird-room: layout

Figure 37 shows the front elevation of the bird-room. The ventilators shown are of the 'hit and miss' type, with a shutter to enable the ventilator to be opened or closed as required.

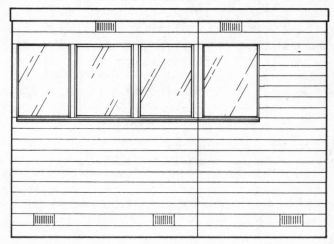

Figure 37 Canary bird-room: front elevation

Figures 38—41 show some of the modules required for the bird-room. The roof and floor modules and the foundations were described in Chapters 3 and 5.

The front of the bird-room is made from a 4 ft (1.2 m) and a 6 ft (1.8 m) wide module, as shown in Figures 38 and 39. The 4 ft (1.2 m) module has one fixed window. Note the position of the ventilators and the supporting framework. The 6 ft (1.8 m) module has three windows: one fixed and two opening. Remember that you require a stay for the bottom of each window and that the window opening should be covered with wire netting, to prevent escapes when the window is open. The rear wall of the bird-room consists of two similar-sized modules, but these are completely clad in timber.

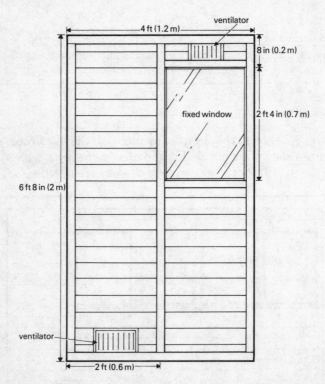

Figure 38 Canary bird-room: 4 ft (1.2 m) window module

Figures 40 and 41 show the door and end wall modules. These complete the perimeter of the bird-room.

The roof and floor can also be made in 6 ft (1.8 m) and 4 ft (1.2 m) modules. It is important to insulate and line the walls and the roof of a canary bird-room. The birds will spend their lifetimes inside the bird-room and it is essential that conditions can be maintained at an even temperature, with fresh air and freedom from damp and draughts. Lighting and heating should be provided if necessary.

A final touch, which aids cleaning as well as improving appearance, is to lay plastic floor covering. This may be considered a luxury, but the flooring is much easier to keep clean than bare boards.

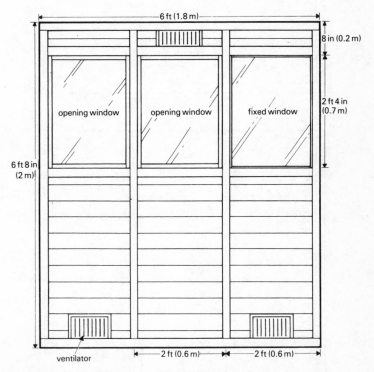

Figure 39 Canary bird-room: 6 ft (1.8 m) window module

Overleaf:
Figure 40 Canary bird-room: 6 ft (1.8 m) door module; view from inside
Figure 41 Canary bird-room: 6 ft (1.8 m) end wall module

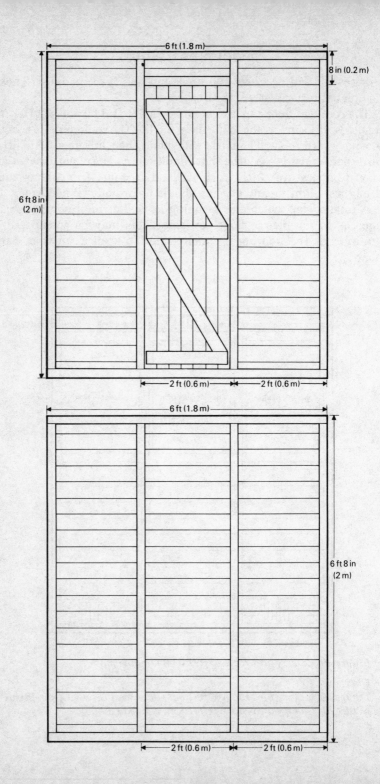

General purpose aviary

Figure 42 shows the layout of a typical general purpose aviary, suitable for budgerigars, zebra finches or foreign birds. The design provides only limited window space and is therefore only suitable for birds which can have access to external flights for the most part of the year.

The aviary consists of a 10 × 6 ft (3 × 1.8 m) bird-room, with two external flights, each 9 × 6 ft (2.7 × 1.8 m). Two internal flights can be provided in the bird-room, each 2 ft (0.6 m) wide by 6 ft (1.8 m) long. Up to eight 3 ft (0.9 m) long breeding cages can be positioned on the rear wall between the flights, with some storage space beneath.

Figure 43 shows the front elevation of the aviary. The position of the door and windows is dictated by the need to provide internal flights at each end of the bird-room. Figures 44−46 show some of the modules required to construct the bird-room. Note the position of the ventilators.

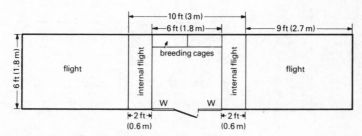

Figure 42 General purpose aviary: layout

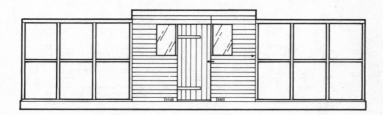

Figure 43 General purpose aviary: front elevation

As in the canary bird-room, a 6 ft (1.8 m) and a 4 ft (1.2 m) wide timber-clad module are needed to form the rear wall of the bird-room. The roof and floor also consist of a 6 ft (1.8 m) and a 4 ft (1.2 m) standard module. The walls and roof should be insulated and lined.

The interior of the bird-room needs some description.The two internal flights require fronts which present two problems. Firstly the front obviously must be constructed to fit the dimensions of the bird-room and this entails measuring the interior of the bird-room when constructed; this is not an easy task as diagonals must be measured to ensure a proper fit. Secondly, if the flight front is constructed in one piece, it is difficult to manoeuvre through the door. The answer to both these problems is to make the front in two pieces, as shown in Figure 47. The module shown, which contains

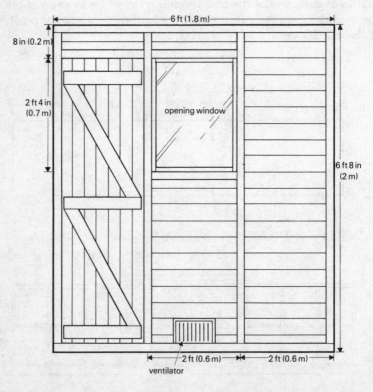

Figure 44 General purpose aviary: 6 ft (1.8 m) door module

the door, has a framework of 1½ × 1 in (38 × 25 mm) timber and is meant to be fitted nearest the windows. The height 'x' is taken from the interior dimension of the bird-room. A gap of about 2 ft 6 in (0.75 m) should then be left. This should be covered with a sheet of ¼ in (6 mm) plywood, which can easily be cut to the correct shape. A length of 1½ × 1 in (38 × 25 mm) timber must be screwed to the rear wall to provide a fixing point for the plywood. The plywood, besides completing the flight front, serves as the side of the breeding cages and also screens the breeding birds from distraction by birds left in the flight. Note that the two flight fronts will be mirror images of each other. Perches can be fitted at each end of the flight and a small shelf should be erected under the pop-hole to hold food and water supplies.

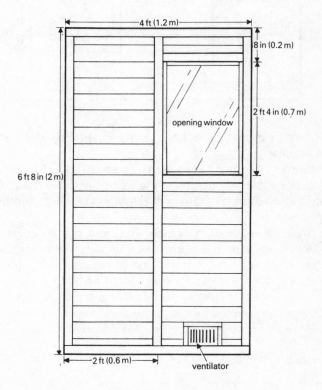

Figure 45 General purpose aviary: 4 ft (1.2 m) window module

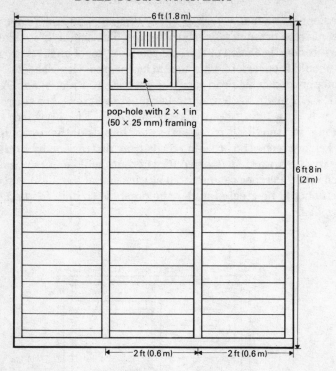

The breeding cages can be 'built-in' (see Chapter 6), with a storage area underneath.

Lighting and heating I consider to be essential as both budgerigars and zebra finches are bred in the early months of the year and, if foreign birds are kept, they will require extra light and heat to stay in condition.

The flights are quite straightforward and can be constructed either from the standard modules (see Chapter 3) or in one piece for economy. A note of caution if you decide to take the latter course! The standard module allows for maximum flexibility in rearranging your aviary, and most people will do this more than once. It also simplifies repairs should netting or woodwork need replacing. The choice is yours, but it needs careful consideration.

Individual breeding aviary

Figure 48 shows an individual breeding aviary suitable for one pair of British or foreign birds. These aviaries can be erected in rows,

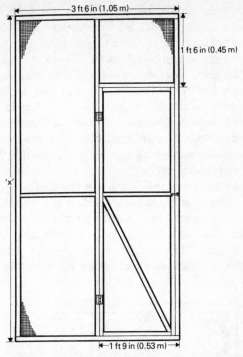

3 ft 6 in (1.05 m)

1 ft 6 in (0.45 m)

'x'

1 ft 9 in (0.53 m)

Figure 46 General purpose aviary: Figure 47 General purpose aviary:
           6 ft (1.8 m) wall module   internal flight module

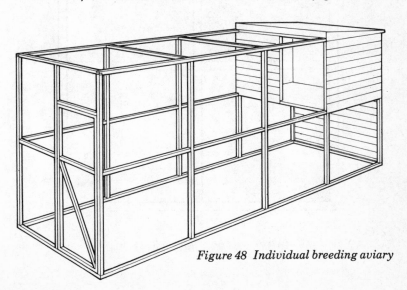

Figure 48 Individual breeding aviary

each additional aviary requiring only one side. The aviary thus consists of a flight with an integral shelter. The birds will normally have their nesting site outside the shelter, the shelter providing a refuge before breeding commences and also a convenient, dry place in which to place food and water. In this case there is no need to continue the shelter to the ground. The half depth shelter is quite adequate and, in fact, if the shelter were continued to ground level it could prove to be dangerous, as birds sometimes find it difficult to fly up from such narrow confines. The area under the shelter provides a suitable nesting site, as it is protected from the weather and from outside disturbances.

Figure 49 shows an inside view of the shelter side module, which forms the rear half of an aviary side wall. It will be seen that one quarter of the module is covered with matching to form the side of the shelter. The matching is fixed on the outside of the framework, with the wire netting, which covers the rest of the module,on the inside. Two modules are required, each a mirror image of the other.

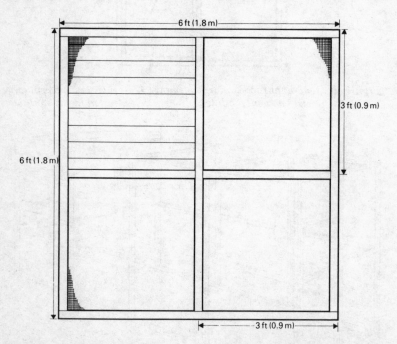

Figure 49 Individual breeding aviary: shelter side module: view from inside

Figure 50 illustrates the shelter back module. This is completely clad in matching. Note the hinged flap, which comes within the confines of the shelter. The purpose of this flap is to provide an access point to the shelter through which food and water may be introduced without entering the aviary. This is an important facility during the breeding season, when disturbance to breeding pairs must be reduced to a minimum. The flap is best hinged at the top so that if the catch is not secured for any reason there is a good chance that the flap will not be open sufficiently for the birds to escape.

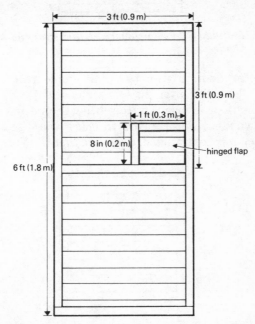

Figure 50 Individual breeding aviary: shelter back module: view from inside

The shelter front module is shown in Figure 51. This provides a half open front to the shelter. The large opening encourages the birds to use the shelter and also allows enough light to enter to overcome the need for a window. Provided the aviary is located sensibly there should be no problem with rain being driven into the shelter. This type of aviary is not suitable for housing foreign birds throughout the winter, although the majority of British birds should find the shelter adequate.

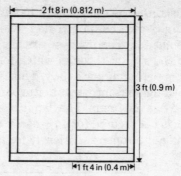

Figure 51 Individual breeding aviary: shelter front module: view from inside

The shelter floor, Figure 52, is a simple rectangular panel, designed to be fitted after the four walls of the shelter have been erected. The floor is inserted from beneath and fixed in place by means of wood-screws. Be sure to check the dimensions of the shelter when it is constructed, to ensure that the floor is a good fit.

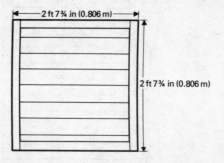

Figure 52 Individual breeding aviary: shelter floor: view from beneath

The roof module, Figure 53, is made to the standard design. If you intend to build a block of these aviaries then do not fix the roofing felt until last.

Figures 54—56 show the flight modules. Note that you will require two flight wall modules for a single aviary, but each additional aviary joined on will require only one.

The aviary can be erected on a low wall foundation, as previously described. The floor of an aviary of this size is best covered with shingle, which can be cleaned by hosing down and easily replaced.

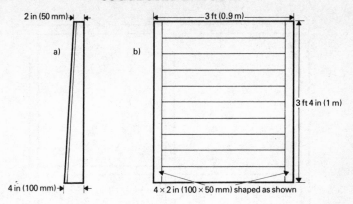

2 in (50 mm)

a)   b)

3 ft (0.9 m)

3 ft 4 in (1 m)

4 in (100 mm)

4 × 2 in (100 × 50 mm) shaped as shown

Figure 53 Individual breeding aviary: shelter roof module: a) end view b) side view

Plants and bushes, which can be essential for nesting sites, should be in containers, so that they can be removed or replaced if the need arises. Grass turfs can be fitted into plastic seed trays so that they can be removed and allowed to recover when they become soiled or damaged.

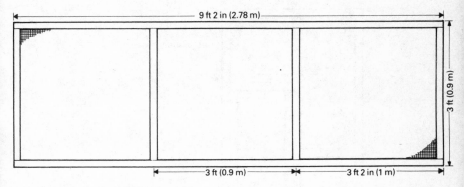

9 ft 2 in (2.78 m)

3 ft (0.9 m)

3 ft (0.9 m)   3 ft 2 in (1 m)

Figure 54 Individual breeding aviary: flight roof module

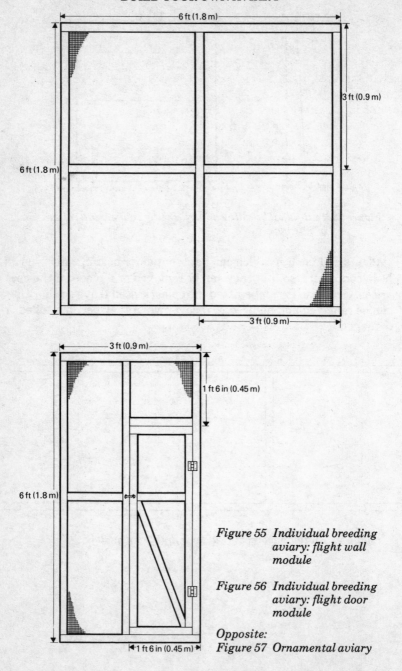

Figure 55 Individual breeding aviary: flight wall module

Figure 56 Individual breeding aviary: flight door module

Opposite:
Figure 57 Ornamental aviary

Ornamental aviary

An ornamental aviary provides a centre of interest and adds to the attraction of any garden. Even if you are already dedicated to one branch of bird-keeping, such an aviary can provide relaxation from the more serious side of you hobby.

The aviary described (see Figure 57) is hexagonal in shape. Thus it can be viewed from any angle and be placed in almost any position in the garden, which is a great advantage.

There are a number of problems to be overcome in constructing an aviary of this type and I have tried to solve these in as simple a manner as possible. Firstly, the adjoining uprights in the framework must be at an angle to the horizontal members, due to the hexagonal shape of the aviary. Secondly, the design and construction of the roof can become complicated. In many designs, the roof of an octagonal aviary comes to a point in the centre. It is, in effect, cone-shaped. This type of roof can be difficult to construct and so I have shown a simple, flat roof which is equally effective.

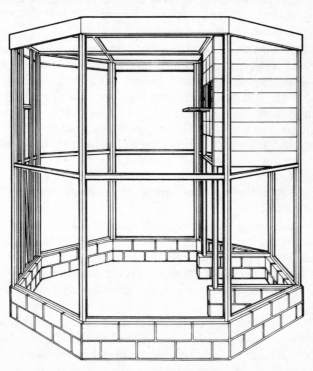

Lastly, there is the question of the shelter. The attraction of the octagonal aviary lies in its shape. If the shelter is placed outside the aviary it spoils the effect and can look like something tacked on as an afterthought. Siting the shelter inside the aviary does present problems, particularly with the roof. From an aesthetic point of view, the shelter should be placed in the middle of the aviary, but in an aviary of this size the flight space is excessively reduced. The position shown for the shelter, at the side of the aviary, is probably the best compromise possible.

The aviary is constructed in modular form. You will need to make six side modules, one door module, one shelter module, a roof, plus the various shelter sections. The framework is constructed from 1½ × 1 in (38 × 25 mm) timber (except for the roof where 3 × 1 in (75 × 25 mm) section is used). In this case 1½ × 1 in (38 × 25 mm) timber is quite adequate as far as structural strength is concerned and is more suited to the shape of framework required. The shelter is clad in 4 × ½ in (100 × 12 mm) matching. The mesh size of the wire netting depends upon the species of birds you wish to keep, but I suggest that ½ in (12 mm) wire netting or 1 × ½ in (25 × 12 mm) 'Twilweld' is a good size to adopt.

The side modules are made first, as these are the easiest to construct. Reference to Figure 58 shows that three horizontal members are required, cut to the shape shown in the enlarged view. Note that the 3 ft (0.9 m) dimension refers to the front edge of the horizontal member. Any form of lap jointing is not practical in this case and the framework can be assembled by using wood screws and a waterproof adhesive, such as Cascamite, to form the joints. Treat the woodwork with a wood preservative before fixing the wire netting. Creosote or a coloured preservative are ideal for the purpose. Remember that both are toxic and do not allow splashes to reach the skin.

Before attaching the netting, nail scrap timber across the corners of the framework to hold it square, while pulling the netting into position. Staples are used to fix the netting, which should be pulled as taut as possible. The cut edges of the netting should be covered. Builder's laths can be used, as before, or strips cut from scrap timber.

The shelter back module is constructed next. The framework is identical to the side module framework, the only difference being the top 3 ft (0.9 m) of the shelter module, which is clad with 4 × ½ in

(100 × 12 mm) matching. Note that the netting should be fitted before the matching.

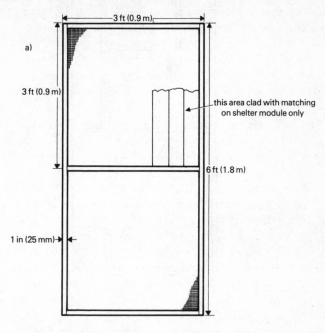

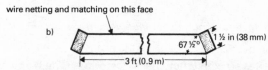

Figure 58 Ornamental aviary: side module: a) front view b) enlarged plan view. Note that the matching must be fitted vertically to the inside of the framework.

The final link in the hexagon is the door module. Reference to Figure 59 will show that the outer framework is identical to that of other modules. The door itself requires two vertical supports at the correct angle to the door frame. This arrangement is achieved by placing the door in the centre of the module. The door frame has a diagonal brace in the lower section as shown. Fit the wire netting as before. The door is shown hung on the right-hand side, but the frame can be reversed if required. A small sliding catch should be fitted to hold the door closed.

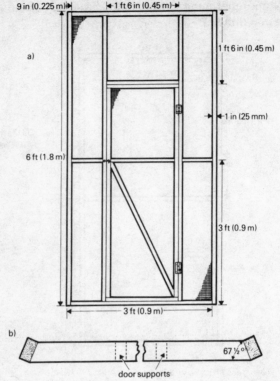

Figure 59 Ornamental aviary: door module: a) front view b) enlarged plan view

The next task is to construct the roof module. The framework for the roof is constructed from 3 × 1 in (75 × 25 mm) timber, with the longer dimension aligned vertically. Four sections of 3 × 1 in (75 × 25 mm), each 7 ft 8 in (2.3 m) long are cut to act as cross pieces. Lap joints are made to produce the arrangement shown in Figure 60. Take careful note of the dimensions and the points from which they are taken. Glue and screw the lap joints together and then fix the four 3 ft 2 in (0.95 m) members across the ends of the cross pieces. The remaining four sections, shown in the diagonal positions in the diagram, are cut to a length of 3 ft 2 in (0.95 m) and the ends cut at 45° to fit. The enlarged view shows the method of fixing. A piece of 1 × 1 in (25 × 25 mm) timber, 3 in (75 mm) long, is cut in half diagonally along its length. This gives a triangular-shaped block which is glued and pinned in position to give added strength to the joint. The joint is completed by glueing and screwing the diagonal member into position. The framework can now be treated with wood preservative.

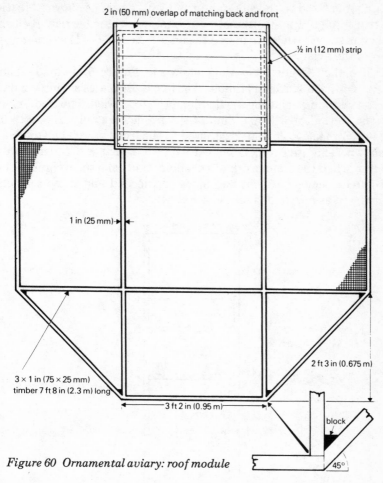

Figure 60 Ornamental aviary: roof module

Next the wire netting should be fixed to the top of the framework, except in the area which is to be covered with matching. This area forms the roof of the shelter. The disadvantage with a flat roof of this type is the poor drainage. The matching is fitted as shown, with a 2 in (50 mm) overlap at back and front. Treat the matching with wood preservative and allow it to dry. The roofing felt can now be fitted, preferably using a roofing compound to stick the felt to the matching. Allow the felt to hang down about 3 in (75 mm) at the back. This provides a guide for the rainwater to drip away from the shelter back. To complete the roof, a strip of ½ × ¼ in (12 × 6 mm) timber is fixed to the sides and front of the roof as shown. Mastic strip is placed under the strip to make a water barrier. By this means the rainwater is forced to run off the back of the roof, away from the aviary.

The shelter side framework shown in Figure 61 is made from 1½ × 1 in (38 × 25 mm) timber. The two cross pieces are intended to act as a fixing point for the floor and the food shelf. The cladding is fixed to the top 3 ft (0.9 mm) of the framework only. A length of 1½ × 1 in (38 × 25 mm) is screwed to the front vertical member as shown. This gives an L-shaped support which will considerably strengthen the framework at this point and take the weight of the shelter. Remember that two sides are needed and these are constructed as mirror images of each other.

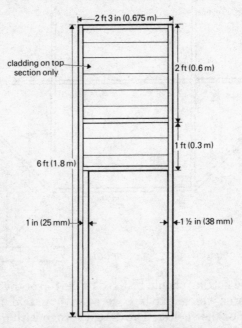

Figure 61 Ornamental aviary: shelter side module

The shelter, of course, needs a floor; this is a simple, rectangular panel, covered with matching (Figure 62). A similar panel is used for the food shelf which is fitted below the shelter. The purpose of this shelf is to provide a dry, sheltered place for the seed, water and other foods.

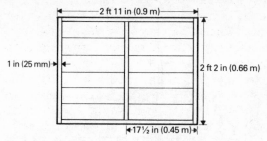

Figure 62 Ornamental aviary: shelter floor and food shelf

The shelter front (Figure 63) is a little more difficult to construct than the other panels, as it contains two windows and a door. Construct the outer framework first and fix the matching in place above and below each window. Each window has a frame formed by the 1½ × 1 in (38 × 25 mm) timber around the opening. A strip of ½ × ¼ in (12 × 6 mm) timber should be nailed all round the rear edge of each window frame to form a seating for the glass. Do not fit the glass until the aviary has been assembled as the size of the glass will depend on the size of the window frames as constructed.

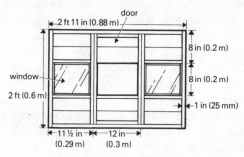

Figure 63 Ornamental aviary: shelter front: view from inside

Measure the aperture and have the glass cut ⅛ in (3 mm) less overall than the size of the aperture. Measure the door aperture as constructed and make the framework for the door. The door also has two pieces of matching above and below the pop-hole. The pop-hole is formed from two pieces of matching held together by two strips of timber on either side, as shown in Figure 64. The flap so formed is hinged at the bottom. With this arrangement the flap will remain in the horizontal position when open. A door bolt can be provided at the top to hold the flap closed.

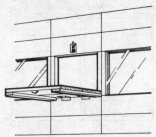

Figure 64 Ornamental aviary: pop-hole and windows

The door is mounted on two hinges and a bolt or similar catch is provided on the opposite side. This door allows access to the interior of the shelter so that it may be cleaned.

This completes the construction of the various modules of the aviary. I have not suggested lining this shelter as its size can cause problems. If you do decide to line it, the dimensions of the modules may have to be adjusted to cater for the thickness of the lining.

The aviary will require a foundation, either a concrete base or a low wall, as shown in Figure 57. The latter method looks much more attractive and gives additional head room inside the aviary. If you stand your aviary on a wall, remember to provide two sections of wall to support the shelter sides. With either method, rag-bolts can be grouted into the wall or concrete to provide fixing points for the aviary.

Erect the sides of the aviary first, fixing the modules together with 1¾ in (43 mm) wood screws. Do not tighten the nuts on the rag-bolts until you have completed the erection of the aviary. Add the roof and secure with wood screws. Next fix the shelter sides. This is the most difficult part of the whole operation. Reference to Figure 65 will show the position of the sides. The front edge of the shelter framework should be in line with the outside edge of the roof framework at that point. It is necessary to cut an angled packing piece as shown. This is cut from a length of 1½ in (38 mm) wide timber and is ⅝ in (16 mm) wide on the inside, tapering to a point. The sides should be screwed to the aviary upright, through the packing pieces, and to the roof framework. It may be necessary to plane the end of the matching at an angle as shown.

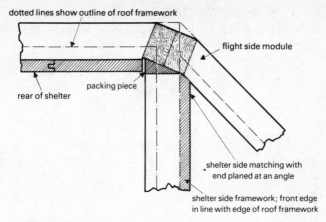

Figure 65   Ornamental aviary: method of fixing shelter sides: view from above

The shelter front can now be attached. A piece of matching 1¾ in (44 mm) wide by 2 ft (0.6 m) long should be nailed to either side of the front to cover the exposed framework at the corners. Add the shelter floor and food shelf and glaze the windows. Tighten the holding-down nuts and make sure that the structure is rigid.

A final touch is to screw lengths of 4 in (100 mm) timber to cover the edge of the roof framework and the top horizontal member of the sides. These sections are added only to improve the appearance of the aviary and can be omitted if you so wish. With the addition of suitable perches and food and water your aviary will then be ready for your birds.

Appendix: Materials required in the construction of bird-rooms and aviaries

Materials	Canary bird-room	General purpose bird-room	Individual breeding aviary	Ornamental aviary
Tongue-and-groove matching:				
4 × ½ in (100 × 12 mm)	950 ft (290 m)	980 ft (300 m)	177 ft (54 m)	150 ft (45 m)
Prepared timber:				
1½ × 1 in (38 × 25 mm)	20 ft (6 m)	—	—	270 ft (81 m)
2 × 1 in (50 × 25 mm)	10 ft (3 m)	10 ft (3 m)	—	—
3 × 1 in (75 × 25 mm)	70 ft (21 m)	10 ft (3 m)	—	60 ft (18 m)
4 × 2 in (100 × 50 mm)		70 ft (21 m)	7 ft (2.25 m)	—
Sawn timber:				
2 × 2 in (50 × 50 mm)	255 ft (78 m)	255 ft (78 m)	280 ft (85 m)	—
Hardwood:				
¼ × ¼ in (6 × 6 mm)	20 ft (6 m)	10 ft (3 m)	—	20 ft (6 m)
½ × ¼ in (12 × 6 mm)	—	—	—	—
Lining material:				
8 × 4 ft (2.4 × 1.2 m)	6 sheets	6 sheets	—	—
Green sand-faced roofing felt	1 roll	1 roll	1 roll	1 roll
Wire netting:				
36 × ½ in (900 × 12 mm)	—	—	60 ft (18 m)	60 ft (18 m)
Netting staples	—	½ lb (0.22 kg)	½ lb (0.22 kg)	½ lb (0.22 kg)
Wire nails: 1 in (25 mm)	1 lb (0.45 kg)	1 lb (0.45 kg)	½ lb (0.22 kg)	½ lb (0.22 kg)
Felt nails	¼ lb (0.11 kg)	¼ lb (0.11 kg)	¼ lb (0.11 kg)	¼ lb (0.11 kg)

Wood screws:				
1¾ in (45 mm)	—	—	—	50
3 in (75 mm)	—	—	—	—
Corrugated fasteners:				
1 in (25 mm)	1 lb (0.45 kg)	1 lb (0.45 kg)	½ lb (0.22 kg)	½ lb (0.22 kg)
Coach bolts:				
5 in (127 mm)	18	18	25	—
Door catch	1	1	—	—
Door bolt	—	4	2	2
Hinges:				
2 in (50 mm), pairs	2	2	2	2
18 in (450 mm), pairs	1	1	—	—
Mastic	Yes	Yes	Yes	Yes
Builders' laths	—	—	42 ft (13 m)	150 ft (46 m)
Roofing compound	1 tin	1 tin	1 tin	1 tin
Glass, cut to requirements	Yes	Yes	—	Yes
Putty	Yes	Yes	—	Yes
Window stays	2	2	—	—
Ventilators-	5	4	—	—
Wood preservative	½ gall (2.5 l)	½ gall (2.5 l)	1 qt (1 l)	1 qt (1 l)
Angle brackets: 3 in (75 mm)	8	8	—	—

N.B. Hinges, bolts, etc. are now usually sold complete with screws. Additional wood screws will be required to suit. Materials for cages, foundations and external flights are dependent upon the method of construction adopted.

Index